CALLAS

CALLAS

Images of a Legend

With an essay by Attila Csampai
Translated by Anne Heritage

Stewart, Tabori & Chang
New York, New York

Contents

The Photographers

Claude Azoulay

Cecil Beaton

Dalmas

John Deakin

Raymond Depardon

Zoe Dominic

John Dominis

Eliot Elisofon

Douglas Glass

Burt Glinn

François Gragnon

Derek Halstead

Horst P. Horst

Jean-Pierre Leloir

Angus McBean

Gerard Neuvecelles

Desmond O'Neill

Gordon Parks

Erio Piccagliani

Edward Quinn

Bill Ray

Willy Rizzo

Houston Rogers

Maurice Sayers

David Seymour

Christian Steiner

Mario Tursi

and many others

Callas

ATTILA CSAMPAI

1. Moments of Eternity

I love him whose soul is lavish, who wanteth no thanks and doth not give back:
for he always bestoweth, and desireth not to keep for himself.

I love him who wanteth to surpass himself and is thereby destroyed.

(Friedrich Nietzsche, *Thus Spake Zarathustra*)

On September 16, 1977, Maria Callas died in her Paris apartment, released from a life that consisted only of lost hopes, disappointments, and wonderful, yet unbearably painful, memories. Born in New York of Greek parents, she had ascended to become Italy's opera queen and conquered the whole world — a magical figure in the "last fairy tale" of our disenchanted times. She gave the world all that an individual can possibly give and more: she surrendered her soul, indeed, her inner universe, thereby exhausting her supreme creative powers. No longer was there a reason for her — the messenger of the gods, the most radiant archangel humankind has yet experienced — to continue living, accompanied only by the tormenting awareness of her past perfection — a fallen angel, maligned and humiliated. Callas the myth and her "fairy tale" message live on, however. And for many her true greatness, her unsurpassed artistry,

her inimitability, has gradually become clear — now that her life of privation, fear, unbending discipline, triumphs, failure, scandals, and extreme shortsightedness lies in the past, and the sensation-hungry reporters who continually plagued and tormented her have grown quiet. Callas knew — and that was her last and only consolation — she was immortal, even if to the very end she yearned and sought to regain what she had forever lost.

Yet, during the ten years of her unquestioned reign, between 1949 and 1959, she bestowed upon the lost souls of the world — disoriented and bewildered by the war — more music, more art, more humanity, and warmth than any other individual of this century. Heaven forbid that we mistake Leonard Bernstein's simple comment — she was "the greatest artist of the world" — for mere flattery. Indeed, she was perhaps the last true artist in an age devoid of myths, artists, and heroes. During Callas's lifetime Ingeborg Bachmann sensed or recognized that "She was the only individual who had a right to stand on a stage in these decades," pointing out the moral and aesthetic superiority of her performances. But not one of the hordes of so-called voice experts and music critics — those who with their fundamental hostility to women, their bourgeois and bureaucratic mentality felt threatened, aesthetically offended, even slighted — has had the courage or even exhibited the musical competence to acknowledge the importance of this singer.

"Everything about her is a matter of opinion," summarized the American Callas-specialist William Weaver with some resignation in the *New York Times* review of a book by the English singer-guru Michael Scott. It is as if the artistic provocation felt even today in her work, so many years after her death, were to make a definitive judgement based on traditional, standardized criteria of vocal aesthetics impossible. For Weaver tends to criticize other aspects of her voice and is not as harsh as his colleague Scott. To this day, Callas still poses a threat to the so-called experts, no longer biographically but artistically. Her art is an incessant declaration of war against the aesthetics of the perfectly balanced register, against the impersonal, flawless, soullessly beautiful tone that can be perceived and examined like an immaculate female figure — prey for men's probing eyes.

Callas was one of the only internationally famous women of this century to become a legendary cult figure without being the idolized object of men's fantasies. All others — Marilyn Monroe, Liz Taylor, Brigitte Bardot, even Dietrich — owe their fame to the rapacious needs of a male society. The traditional typology ranges from *femme fragile* to *femme fatale*, from *La Traviata* to *Lulu*. Callas, however, did not fit these categories; if anything, she was a *femme scandaleuse* — a perpetual scandal — the embodiment of provocation for

the tottering patriarchal society of the fifties. It was not her voice that offended the masses, but her very being, her absolute professionalism, the primacy of a rigorous discipline over her private needs, her artistic perfection, her fighting spirit vis-à-vis an audience that never loved her and had to be won over with her voice again and again: triumphs that brought her no happiness.

She did not instigate the scandals herself, except once after twelve years of marriage when she left her twenty-six year older husband for Aristoteles Onassis. It was the tabloids who stylized her — the uncompromising artist — as the temperamental and notorious prima donna of a puritanical era. Yet it proved to be more of a curse than a boon when in 1953, the year of her worldwide breakthrough, she decided to start slimming, weary of being ridiculed by reviewers — including music critics — as a formless monster, the "prima donna with elephant's legs." She yearned to have a flawless appearance, to be perfect and beautiful. She wasn't interested in attracting men with the sex appeal and curves of a Marilyn Monroe or Jayne Mansfield but rather in turning her inner musical beauty outward — into an aesthetic form like a statue, a consummate beauty, a fairy-tale figure. She wanted to look like Audrey Hepburn — fragile, graceful, ethereal. Within one year, while she was singing the most difficult roles at La Scala and at opera houses in London, Verona, and Rome, she shed over sixty pounds. In just a few months her iron will transformed her appearance so radically that the conductor Carlo Maria Giulini, with whom she had performed Gluck's *Alceste* in Milan not long before, hardly recognized her. Suddenly Callas was photogenic and became, if not an object of desire, a sensation to excite and perturb the masses.

What she achieved musically and dramatically over a period of five or six consecutive years and in tremendously difficult roles was of little interest to the larger public. The masses craved news confirming the cliché of the "tiger" or the "fury." Thus, when she found the courage in Rome on that ominous 2 January 1958 to walk out on a performance of *Norma* attended by the president of Italy because of a sore throat and her feeling of true responsibility toward the work, she was condemned by the press and for all practical purposes declared a *persona non grata*. She became the most hated woman in the world. The invincible had shown her Achilles heel, and now the wounded "beast of prey" could be cornered and hunted down. And suddenly, hitherto *prima donna assoluta* and priestess of the most sublime art, she found herself in the profane and entirely unmusical regions of the diamond-studded demimonde, the nouveaux riches, who, amusing themselves in a decadent, glittering artificial world of pleasure and leisure, lived off the work of others. It was a rigidly structured society, in which women, if they were allowed entry at all, were only valued as status objects.

What was the most disciplined and professional woman artist of this century seeking in this milieu of idlers, hedonists, confidence men, and money-seekers? What could friendship with Elsa Maxwell, the most influential but also the most malicious gossip in America offer her? And what gift could Onassis bestow upon her that she, the best-paid opera singer of the world, could not purchase herself? No one in this circle of soulless lemurs was interested in her singing, her music, her unique artistry — for she was pure art, the incarnate ideal of artistic beauty. Both Elsa Maxwell and Onassis were attracted and fascinated by her fame and the exotic flair of an opera prima donna, who by singing old-fashioned arias when opera was thought to be dead, succeeded in becoming a greater celebrity than all the film stars and prominent figures of the time. Maxwell's reviews were guided purely by her subjective interest; her musical evaluation is

completely worthless. And it is well-known that Callas's few remaining triumphs — the number of performances was drastically reduced after her affair with Onassis began in 1959 — were a threat to his self-esteem. Later he did not even bother to attend her rare appearances and attempted to persuade her to give up singing for acting. He apparently had no inkling of the artistic importance of his world-famous conquest, whom he later exchanged for another dream woman of the masses, Jackie Kennedy.

Nevertheless, neither Onassis, Elsa Maxwell, nor the sensation-hungry press can be held responsible for the rapid decline of her voice after 1959. Callas biographers and critics have often made use of the story as it fits so nicely into the cliché of the "unfaithful" wife whose transgressions are punished by God. But in reality, after years of overtaxing her voice, the first signs of damage were already evident two years before her liaison with Onassis began.

Indeed the incident at the *Norma* performance in Rome on 2 January 1958 sounded the first shrill alarm of her advancing vocal problems. It became a scandal and a personal tragedy for Callas, only because she let herself be pushed onto the stage with an acute sore throat. It was the audience who behaved scandalously — and the president, who, concerned about his reputation, complained of not having been informed in time of her decision. With their own ears they all heard how Callas struggled to finish the first act, and yet not one individual showed any understanding for the courageous decision of the prima donna, whose highly honed artistic sensibility would not allow her to risk losing her voice in the second act.

But such thoughts were no longer of interest to the public inside or outside opera houses. Callas had become too famous, too much a part of high society. In an interesting book on the singer, Jürgen Kesting refers to this phenomenon as her "descent into fame." She now had to play the pathetic and humiliating role of the diva involved in one scandal after the next — mercilessly exposed to the slanderous attacks of an entire horde of hack writers out to demonize their anti-idol and to turn her into the world's most hated woman. If in her defense she had called upon opera tradition or the priority of artistic quality, scorn and derision would have rained upon her. The ovations, the cries of "bravo," the undivided attention of opera-goers gave way to the blood-thirsty carping and shrieking of the mesmerized masses. They wanted to see blood — the sacrificial death of the witch, the woman who dared to challenge and mock the whole world by subjecting the public to her every whim. For she now revealed imperfections, faults, and weaknesses in her hitherto masterful, yet boldly assertive art. The Italians were in a rage and some cried out, "Is she even Italian? What is this foreigner doing in our opera houses, this uncivilized American, who doesn't look after her poor mother in Greece? With her ugly and uncouth voice and her poor Italian husband she married only to be able to sing here?"

This was the thanks for having given humanity every treasure that a human soul can hold, and hers was a vessel, no, an ocean. Mercilessly, like the masses that turned against her, she consumed herself; she rendered up her unique genius, her inner voice, and yet she remained modest and unpretentious, loyal to her art and its demands. No man could have done this without entertaining delusions of grandeur. More than Bellini's *Norma* — of whom she was the quintessential personification — she was a *casta diva*, the chaste and immaculate high priestess of art. And her obsession with God, transfigured into a pure love of mankind — for music is nothing else but gazing inward to one's own godliness — this selflessness was a thorn in the side of the masses.

In her devotion to her art she also offended her colleagues by unintentionally revealing their vocal and musical deficiencies. Many of the supposedly "influential" men in her artistic career — conductors, directors, producers, and opera house directors — experienced her superiority as an affront and threat to their own self-esteem. Walter Legge, for example, the powerful EMI producer and artistic "supervisor" of the majority of Callas's recordings — a man who is generally counted among her most important well-wishers — began his acclaimed obituary in the 1977 November issue of *Opera News* with a completely inappropriate quotation from another Callas supporter, the Italian conductor Tullio Serafin. Looking back on his long career, Serafin once said that he had experienced three miracles — Caruso, Ponselle and Rufo. The distinguished Briton Walter Legge, who was married to another famous opera diva — Elisabeth Schwarzkopf — followed this verdict with a psychoanalytical interpretation of Callas, which in somewhat more refined language paraphrased the nonsense of the tabloids. Callas had suffered "from a superhuman inferiority complex," he claimed, thinking that he had solved the riddle of her life, for, "This was the driving force behind her relentless, ruthless ambition, her fierce will, her monomaniacal egocentricity and insatiable appetite for celebrity. Self-improvement, in every facet of her life and work, was her obsession." Who would have dared to contradict this seemingly competent eye-witness, even if his despicable attempt to interpret her musicality and passionate expressivity as symptoms of an illness could in no way impair the growing Callas legend?

If there were no recordings of Callas, then, I am quite sure, there would have been hosts of influential pharisees judging and condemning her, and finally eliminating her from public memory — a mere false prophet, a minor accident in the history of opera. In Italy, the country in which she appeared in more than 360 performances, such a tribunal was held in 1969 — during her lifetime — by the national broadcasting company. Entitled "Callas's Trial," music critics, such as Rodolfo Celletti, who described her voice as that of a "ventriloquist," but also competent musicians and artists, such as the conductor Gianandrea Gavazzeni, who often worked with Callas, and, unfortunately, Luchino Visconti, her best director, participated in this infamous and embarrassing event. Here, the Italians were able to act out in public their latent aversion to the foreigner Callas, who was not even able to win over a man like Antonio Ghiringhelli, the director of La Scala, after she had made his opera house the center of the opera world. Admittedly, she was not locked up or burnt as a witch as would have happened a few hundred years ago, but she was publicly condemned for fifteen years of "opera transgressions" in the motherland of music and musical theater.

If she had not married the Veronese brick factory owner Giovanni Battista Meneghini, who at the time of their marriage was fifty-three — twice as old as Callas — she would never have achieved her sensational ascent as the *prima donna assoluta* in the conservative, patriarchal society of this Mediterranean peninsula. That the elderly, or even grandfatherly, Meneghini preferred the role of a petty manager to that of a retiring, serious husband did more harm than good to Callas's highly sensitive self-esteem, at least in the eyes of so-called refined circles of opera management and music reviewers. Nevertheless, Meneghini was one of the few men close to Callas whose own self-confidence was not adversely affected by her artistic powers. Thus, during the decisive years of her artistic development he did not hold her back, rather he played the role of the relatively satisfied and patient, simple partner of the career woman whose provincial behavior causes an

occasional faux pas — a role usually allotted to the wives or partners of great men.

No doubt this deviation from the accepted roles in Meneghini and Callas's marriage also angered the prudish post-war society with its repressive attitudes towards women. Thus, millions of Callas loathers smiled with satisfaction when the true ox of a man, Onassis, treated her miserably — exactly the treatment an overbearing woman deserves. And when, after being publicly humiliated, the most famous woman of the fifties was simply discarded in exchange for the most prominent widow of the sixties, the attractive Jackie Kennedy, in the eyes of the public Callas had paid her dues. Hate was transformed into something worse — pity, which in her later performances and concerts appeared to undermine her self-confidence more than the horrific pressures of her success years.

This explains why in 1973, eight years after her last opera performance, she let herself be persuaded by the tenor Giuseppe de Stefano, the third of her three husbands, to undertake a worldwide farewell tour lasting almost thirteen months. And this despite the fact that her voice had deteriorated to such an extent that no trace was left of its one-time splendor. Her partner of many years, who had not once come close to being her equal, was finally able to outsing his completely exhausted prima donna. Her artistic sense, her musicality, seemed to have disappeared and with it her will to live. She was a defenseless and lost individual, now that the gods had abandoned her. What can life still mean to someone who has experienced the divine, carried it within herself, expressed it and, while she sang, was miraculously released from this world, protected by her own musical aura — the consummate sound with the magical power of transforming the private to the universal and thus to the divine.

Callas lost her magical powers and had fallen from the high spheres of the absolute —

absolute beauty and absolute humanity — into the depths of the world, of life, of mortality, and beauty faded to a dream, to a memory. She died of sorrow over this loss. She was perhaps the only woman of this century to pass the threshold separating human life from the sphere of divine art and music: she had penetrated most deeply into this magical kingdom — where the inner spirit of the individual takes on an objective form — as the ancient Greek poet Pindar defined art 2,500 years ago.

In his twelfth Pythian ode Pindar distinguished man's lamenting from its artistic representation in the melody of the aulos (a Greek wind instrument) player. And it was this significant difference in quality that the Greek musicologist Georgiades, at about the same time Callas was appearing worldwide, demonstrated to be at the root of Western musical development: "The goddess Athena was so moved by the lament of Medusa's sister Euryale that she wanted to preserve it. She felt the need to immortalize her impression, to give it an objective form. This overpowering, heart-rending plaintive cry of sorrow was to be represented by, or better, was to be represented as melody. The lamentation was transformed into art, into mastery, into the sound of the aulos, into music. Athena had, as it were, woven the melody from the motifs of human lamentation. Pindar ... separates sorrow from the spiritual vision of sorrow. The one, the emotive act, is human, it is symptomatic of life, it is life itself. But the other, creating an objective form of sorrow in art, is divine, is liberating, is an act of the spirit."

Callas was the only singer of this century, perhaps in entire operatic history, to have given expression in her voice, in the shape of her tones, to this fundamental difference between human suffering and its universal, artistic form, thereby fulfilling the absolute demands of art. Thus, it was not poetic license

when Ingeborg Bachmann wrote, "she [was] the only creature who has ever deserved to stand on the opera stage."

Outside of Bachmann and a few other highly talented artists, such as Bernstein, Karajan, Visconti and Zeffirelli, there was hardly a soul who appreciated her art, hardly anyone who grasped or even sensed the monumentality of her artistry, the heights of her mastery — even amongst those who were close to her and had experienced the long path leading to her perfection. Rather, feelings of amazement, irritation, and negative fascination predominated. Many tried to interpret the genius tormenting her in psychological terms and thus separate it from the historical development of the art of singing, which even today is misunderstood as a continuum of subjects and schooling. Her art, her unbridled will to form, was degraded to a signal, a symptom of a psychic defect resulting from a childhood marred by the vicissitudes of a broken family, emigration, loss of love, war, and hunger. And thus the label of a supposedly "superhuman inferiority complex" was easily attached to her, a label she fought against, unsuccessfully, until her sad death. Her self-confidence, her intelligence, and her unusually developed artistic assessment of others, her natural and unaffected behavior that could not hide her New York childhood, in short, her "emancipated" behavior, was a threat to the arduously-maintained inner countenance of the newly "liberated" post-war society.

Callas was one of the last prominent female victims of the rapidly collapsing delusions of superiority of a worn-out patriarchal society. Physics, visionaries, fools, and saints, who proclaimed the truth or were models for humanity almost always paid with their lives; intelligent women were burnt at the stake before they could even begin to proclaim the truth. Callas saw her chance in creating something beyond herself, and in the process she slowly destroyed herself.

And none of her many new young fans, who, like myself, have heard only her recordings, dare think today would be any different from the prudish fifties. With today's digital technology, the acoustic quality of some of her live recordings would be considerably better. But in the completely commercialized opera business an unusual voice like hers would have less chance today than it did forty years ago. Similarly, the tabloids are no less squeamish, and the general taste and level of education of the audiences as well as the critics has declined even more, almost reaching its nadir. Those who have followed the continuing discussion of her vocal defects can imagine the attacks that such a provocative loner would expect today from the critics, that miserable, arrogant, semi-literate, tasteless and above all unmusical mob whose spokesmen dare to place singers like Ileana Cotrubas or Jessye Norman above her. Let us therefore be happy that there are so many excellent studio recordings and even more live recordings that make the difference evident and prevent us from making even greater fools of ourselves than the audiences of her time. Orpheus would not have a chance in our times.

2. Art, Medium, and the Message

"The Oracle of Delphi"

(Margherita Wallmann on Maria Callas)

"Callas Athena"

(*Spiegel* headline)

The gods are silent, but the angels sing. No other human being sang like her, no earthly being. IT sang through her. IT: the gods, primal knowledge, the powers of the universe. The tone glowed in her like lava, red glowing lava. And as soon as she sounded the note, it became mysteriously airborne, growing until it become palpable, filling every corner of the room, enveloping her in a protective aura that separated her from the world. It dazzled our souls as the sun blinds our eyes, inflamed our hearts and warmed our spirits like the voice of an archangel who announces the Last Judgment — so powerful, so deep, so exalted. It was the sound of the high, elevated tone that vibrates in the Word of God made comprehensible as a message between souls. Callas was the only medium ever to step onto the stage and indeed the "only being" that has ever deserved to stand on the stage, as Ingeborg Bachmann, after having seen her once, decreed.

How can a traditional, utterly superficial, positivistic and bourgeois aesthetic possibly comprehend such a semi-goddess, a messenger from the other world, a Greek oracle? It would be the same as explaining the movements of the universe with planimetry. Who would earnestly endeavor to interpret her message from heaven as a series of more or less successful notes? Only morons would do so, narrow-minded, ignorant, insensitive, musical dimwits, believers in the Ptolemaic system, nit-pickers, land surveyors, and cynics who believe only in tangible reality. From the beginning of Callas's career, they dominated the scene and even today continue to criticize her voice — its lack of beauty, its unevenness, its roughness. Since when, I wonder, does the judgment of the majority about art carry more weight than the competency and perceptive ability of a few? Callas is a test for the level of education, the insight, and musicality of a whole era. And in the eyes of future generations, I believe, the Callas critics will not fare well.

What the so-called experts have published in their analyses of her vocal imperfections in the last thirty years has revealed more about the limits and shortcomings of the entire discipline than it sheds light on the nature of Callas's voice. But how meaningful is an aesthetics of singing that preaches "the balance of register" and seeks above all to eliminate individual expression and coloring, choosing to ignore the mystery of human singing, and to reduce it to its purely instrumental aspects as if the voice were a wind instrument. This view cultivates a flawless, technical beauty — an artificial, inhuman, soulless tone without emotional reverberations, without unevenness and imperfections — a female voice which sings like a mechanical bird.

Maurice Ravel once commented that he preferred to listen to the song of an artificial bird because he could hear its heart beat. This merely expresses his skepticism towards a lifeless aesthetic applied primarily to women singers. Why grant a woman on stage the ability to do what she has been denied for hundreds or thousands of years — not only to think and act independently but also to feel deeply?

The inner life of women was overlooked until well into the nineteenth century either because it was safely hidden behind a taboo or declared to be non-existent. The pressure to accept a subordinate role and to follow social patterns of passivity precluded the idea, at least in the eyes of men, of women being passionate. Accordingly, even well into the twentieth century their spectrum of vocal expression was limited in comparison with that of men; the physical and social superiority of a man's voice was not by any means to be infringed upon. Today one can hear the strangely old-fashioned, throaty, squeaky sound of repression and subordination on numerous old recordings of great singers from the turn of the century up to the twenties and thirties. There was a threshold of inhibition — a taboo supported by stylistic theories — which women were not allowed to overstep. Callas alone broke away from this tradition through the power, the intensity, fullness, and "masculine" diction of her tone, provoking the male-dominated society more than through political statements. She brought the 350-year supremacy of men on the stage to its knees, so to speak, at a time, of course, when opera was considered at its end, and even performances were endangered. Callas was a major factor in the rising post-war popularity of opera, and she has ensured its survival to this very day. Similarly, by making numerous studio recordings that were to set new standards, she helped establish the possibilities of the long-playing record as a second, new medium for the old genre opera: Malraux' *musée imaginaire* — the musical fantasy stage of the record.

Indeed, it is because there are so many records of her (and new live recordings of her stage performances are still being discovered) documenting her artistic uniqueness that her successors must struggle to establish themselves. The musical standards she set can now be verified, and anyone, using an analog or digital "time machine" can listen to her without having to depend on the judgment of others. This is also one reason why so many established music critics remain skeptical to this day toward recordings for they destroy their privileged position as mediators of art.

Several of the archconservative proponents of the old gentlemen's club of vocal experts who proudly proclaim "to have been there" use this biological advantage as an argument against young Callas fans, maintaining that only those who have seen and heard her on stage can judge her. May the sword of the eyewitnesses blind the author of these lines! The Callas skeptics of the older generation, however, will find consolation in the fact that of the many precocious yuppies who never experienced her live, the Callas enthusiasts are clearly in the minority.

I have already mentioned that in the fifties it was nevertheless possible for a unique artist like Callas to establish herself despite Meneghini, Onassis, the hatred of her colleagues and sometimes her audience, and the materialistic post-war mentality. I fear that today this would no longer be possible. The greatly increased economic tempo generates other idols: short-lived, undemanding stars brought up on fast food and simulated on the computer screen — without inner substance, without magic, without music, models of humans with synthetic bodies and no feelings, whose jerky movements are controlled from a source outside of themselves.

Can one imagine a greater contrast to the slow, measured movements of Callas on stage, which, according to many competent observers, always gave the impression of utmost mobility. Similarly when she sang, even at a cutting fortissimo, she was relying on only a small part of her voice. She had dignity, the dignity of an antique myth; she was sacrosanct and unapproachable. She was burning the candle at both ends, but who would have dared to extinguish this holy fire. When she sang she did not accept any contradictions, and she cast a spell over everyone, including her enemies. And when she occasionally flung her accusations in the face of her audience, then even the claques were silent. At moments like these, according to eye-witnesses, it was as if judgment day had arrived, and the audience reacted as if they were strangely uneasy. The ovations that exploded afterwards only confirmed the renewed triumph of the fearless Jeanne d'Arc over the dark, anonymous powers.

Callas — she had the most radical and fanatic will to create, to make truth tangible — the abstract idea of truth which finally takes on the shape of beauty. True beauty is all-encompassing, it does not exclude the other. And her voice was exactly that: light and dark, soft and hard, warm and cold, visible and invisible, day and night, idea and substance, movement and form, heaven and hell. She enacted the message of the gods to mankind: the beauty of art is superior to the beauty of nature.

Is there a more splendid example of the transformation of a nondescript, shapeless bundle of complexes, an ugly Cinderella, into the most beautiful, radiant, and noble queen? With her extreme determination, instinct, musicality and artistic understanding, this woman literally created herself. Out of her semi-precious material she created the most beautiful jewel; like the brightest diamond and the deepest sapphire she caught the light of the sun and directed it towards us. Like a blind visionary, a prophet, or an oracle, she saved, from the gray and faded zone of the past, messages from heaven and hell — the long forgotten and repressed truths — and rediscovered mankind's deepest characteristic: pure and undisguised emotion, stripped of its historical and social dimensions. She gave expression in the purest, deepest, and most moving form to human grief and, above all, to woman's lamentation, the song of the loving wife whose emotion reaches much deeper — to the source of the universe — than the naive, child-like cry of Orpheus lamenting his loss.

Callas — she was the most civilized, artistic, humane and purest expression of humanity, the fulfilled being. She achieved an all-surpassing artistry of form and expression. No one could have imagined a mortal being capable of creating such a magical tone. No other human being has delved so far into the kingdom of absolute art, of absolute expression. Callas was truly the first being who rightfully stepped onto the stage. And everyone who was on the stage with her was lost. Not because she tried to point out their poverty of expression but because her tone was so much fuller, intensive, colorful, and authentic.

And even at the end, when her voice had left her, the dark magical powers were still there — for example, in her disquieting portrayal of Princess Eboli. Callas could afford not to cover up her weaknesses. Masterpieces are relatively immune to the external signs of deterioration. This is true of Greek statues, antique ruins, Leonardo's *Last Supper,* and numerous great frescoes. In the ruins of her voice the lasting remains of its former greatness were audible, the unforgettable memory of an unrivalled vocal and musical power.

Was it a typically female voice, did it have the bright, flattering color that immediately triggers the male hunting instinct? No, never. Her voice had a solid and dense structure, with, at least in the early years, austere contours. This was not the voice of a weak woman, it was the trumpets of Jericho, the attempt to go beyond the natural limits of the female voice, to capture the entire range of human expression, to create the quintessential human lamentation. Her voice was a palace; in it, all emotions, feelings, and affects had a home. There were no promptings of the heart, no passions, no sentiments — except the purely animalistic — for which the appropriate color was missing from her inexhaustible palette. She insisted on the totality of emotions and sought in each and every note, in each ornament, its dramatic meaning and truth. Until the very last she believed that the sole purpose of singing is to portray the human soul as convincingly as possible. Art without a concrete motive, without the inner drive of pain or passion was not possible for her. Thus, she abolished with one fell swoop the laws of female singing that had existed for over two hundred years and established her own, emancipatory idea of beauty: art was subordinate to truth. Only the truth, only the authentic can be transformed into beauty. The agility and flexibility of her voice is proof that beauty always entails movement, vitality, and the flow of energy. Her voice was an affront to death, to everything morbid and stationary.

Technocrats still complain that she had three different voices and I respond: she had a thousand voices, but she always selected the appropriate one to express the truth. Her voice was an orchestra — all the possible female tessitura down to a tenor. Or what range do the low notes belong to in the "Suicidio!" from *Gioconda,* which she sang in dark, austere tones as no other woman has ever achieved? She was a chameleon, the most universal of artists, who like every great actor and actress is able to assume any role without losing their individual character traits. Callas's voice had many sides, but it always remained her voice, distinctively hers; it kept its individual character and in terms of the totality and intensity of expression was to the very last beyond comparison. That a colorless singer like Renata Tebaldi could be seen as Callas's main "rival," a kind of gentle alternative to the Greek "tiger," throws, after twenty years, a suspicious light on the musical competence of the critics and on the whole era. Tebaldi and all the others who were cast as Callas rivals by the male-dominated musical scene represent, of course, the preferred image of the obedient, passive, well-mannered woman, who, also in her musical expression, does not step beyond the limits of society. Callas broke this taboo — only for the sake of art, of course, — but no man could comprehend this, except for a few bi- and homosexual artists.

The masses were offended, and thus they pushed Callas into the role of the fighting woman, Jeanne d'Arc, but even more into that of the antique hero, who assailed the entire male society and immobilized it until her powers dissipated. Her only crime was that she served art, fulfilled her mission, obeyed the powers on high. As Ingeborg Bachmann said, "She was always art ... and she was always human, always the poorest, the most afflicted, the Traviata."

As a musical medium Callas had a very concrete idea of consummate artistic form. Strictly speaking, she was not an interpreter of music, seeking the ultimate form of expression. She strove for the absolute and had the technique and the knowledge to achieve it. If interpretation is seen as one possibility among many, then Maria Callas surpassed this level of approach in almost all her roles, for she sought and took on the identity of the figure. In which of her roles did she not immediately create *the* authentic figure, bringing the past history of operatic interpretation to a sudden close? Name a Lucia, a Norma, a Tosca, a Violetta, a Medea, a Leonora, an Elvira or Rosina that is more authentic than that of Callas. She played the roles to their end, thought them through to their end, sang them to their end. She was the climax and the turning point of Western singing. After her the art of singing has experienced its decline: the voice has succumbed to commercialism and its aesthetic standards lost.

She came from nowhere; she had no predecessors and no successors. The world has grown darker since she left — quiet, barren, robbed of her secrets. Her records are all that remains — did I say "all?" We should fall on our knees and thank all her fans who dared to record her stage performances. They are the most beautiful love letters that a woman could leave to mankind. The acoustic museum of her art is indestructible — the only shield against ignorance, incompetence and unmusicality. On this stage of our imagination she still touches our souls with her humanity and continues to defy — now from a higher vantage point — death.

3. Metamorphoses

*It is the Queen of Sheba who is passing! The Empress of China and the Czarina
of Russia! It is the Queen of Spain! It is Cleopatra! It is Aida. Double the
trumpets. Quadruple the fanfare! It is all the queens and empresses at once!*

*Who could have resisted this voice! Hypnotized, I steered my boat straight ahead
to be dashed to pieces on the rocks of the Lorelei! I was in love!*
Yves Saint-Laurent

Macbeth. La Scala, 7 December 1952.

Inauguration of the new opera season. Callas, just turned twenty-nine and weighing over 230 pounds, is on her way to becoming the *prima donna assoluta* of Italy. It is her third Scala premiere.

Shakespeare's Lady Macbeth — intelligent, ambitious, and childless — goes mad in middle age. Today she would be an entrepreneur, a politician, a model — a successful career woman without children. In the past she was either married or in a convent (or burnt at the stake). If married, she invested all her energy in her husband's career, supported and encouraged him, become his inner demon, a second, more powerful ego. Shakespeare's fable is about this fateful liaison: the strong and gifted woman on the side of the weak and indecisive man, a marriage of negative dependencies, of complementary symptoms. Verdi saw in Shakespeare's drama the opportunity to incor-
porate illness, madness, i.e. real life, into opera, albeit using a completely intact musical language. Yet how is it possible to sing something that is incompatible with singing? An ailment of the soul cannot be expressed by beautiful singing. In a famous letter to Salvatore Cammarano, who was in charge of the premiere in Naples, Verdi wrote: "Tadolini is very attractive, but I want Lady Macbeth to be ugly and evil. Tadolini sings perfectly, but I don't want Lady Macbeth to sing. Tadolini has an outstanding, clear, bright, and powerful voice, and I want Lady Macbeth to have a raw, choking, hollow voice. Tadolini's voice is angel-like; the voice of Lady Macbeth should have something of the devil in it . . ."

Verdi would have to wait 105 years before the singer appeared who was capable of capturing this paradoxical aesthetics, this contradiction between outer harmony and inner disharmony, this poisoned bel canto. Maria

Callas sang the role in just one series of five performances and never again. But this was sufficient to set a standard that is yet to be surpassed.

The climax of this opera is in Act IV, the famous sleepwalking scene, in which Verdi, in his quest to revitalize Romantic opera, went beyond the psychologically less sophisticated mad scenes of his predecessors Bellini and Donizetti. Tormented by compulsive sleepwalking, Lady Macbeth dies of madness — a typical female figure in a male-dominated society, who with her naive ability to suppress her own desires finds an outlet for her neurotic energy in her will to dominate her husband. Macbeth, on the other hand, is doomed because of his destructive paranoia. In Shakespeare's drama these two distinctive forms of madness, one characteristic of men, the other of women, were fully developed long before modern psychoanalysis. And Verdi also adopts Shakespeare's humanistic perspective by including two minor figures in the opera: the doctor and Lady Macbeth's maid. It is through their comments that a one-sided view of the events is avoided; instead of superstitious amazement or pure horror, Lady Macbeth is seen through the eyes of the doctor (present during the mad scene) as a creature to be pitied, someone mentally ill who needs to be cared for. And this is why Verdi composed the most beautiful and tender music for her death scene — in its long instrumental introduction reminiscent of Violetta Valéry, another ill, pitiable operatic figure. Verdi felt that this aria, with its dissonances and agonizing grace notes, should not be sung. But how? How can one express, articulate, sing the silent, inner truth of a dream? A singing sleepwalker? Isn't Verdi demanding the impossible of a singer?

The question would still be unanswered if Maria Callas had not proved on 7 December 1952 and on four other evenings that it is possible. Her successors have either not attempted to step beyond the narrow limits of bel canto or in their attempt to imitate Callas they have faltered. Fiorenza Cossotto simply ignored the stage directions; she sang powerfully, as if awake and completely alert, but with the same inner detachment as in the previous three acts. Leonie Rysanek relied on a darker timbre of her not particularly demonic-sounding voice and embellished the whole with a powerful downward thrust of her chest tones. Mara Zampieri's interpretation was impeded by the slow tempi of the conductor Giuseppe Sinopoli, forcing her to overemphasize each note, giving the whole performance an unintentionally comic effect. Shirley Verrett also suffered under the sluggish tempi of Maestro Abbado. She made the mistake of appearing mysteriously demonic at her death although in this last minute of truth she should have revealed her inner madness. The other Lady Macbeths on record — whether Leyla Gencer, Grace Bumbry, Sylvia Sass, Birgit Nilsson or Elena Souliotis — have all capitulated to the aesthetic demands of the sleepwalking scene. Callas's interpretation remains singular and inimitable; she is the only one who was capable of rendering the letter and the spirit of Verdi's score. If we didn't know that Callas made opera history in numerous other roles, we could say without hesitation: Maria Callas *is* Lady Macbeth.

Lucia di Lammermoor, Berlin, Staatsoper, 29 September 1955.

Guest performance of the Scala company with Herbert von Karajan conducting. In addition to Victor de Sabata and Bernstein, Karajan was one of the few directors who was not intimidated by her genius, who could inspire her artistically to even higher feats. Tullio Serafin, her much-touted mentor, was her best Italian conductor, but he merely followed her lead, he did not offer enough resistance, he could not curb her effusive tendencies. No one, not even Arturo Toscanini, was able to bridle her spirit; it had to be prodded, even forced, to the highest artistic expression by a tender and flexible, yet powerful hand. And this optimal constellation let the Berlin performance culminate in one of the most beautiful, unforgettable moments of opera history.

Act III, Scene I, the mad scene, Part II. Cabaletta. A "cheerful" departure from a gloomy life that led to madness: *Spargi d'amaro pianto il mio terrestre velo, mentre lassù nel cielo io pregherò, pregherò, per te ... Al giunger tuo soltanto fia bello il ciel per me!* It isn't necessary to read the score; Callas articulates the notes and the spoken text so perfectly that they once again assume their original purpose as performance instructions — an abstract approximation of musical and expressive form. Callas succeeds here in transforming the text and notes into musical fantasy and tone, into a pure anthropomorphic form. An artistic figure is transformed into a human being.

Komm, süßer Tod, du bist mein Freund. How is it possible to entice one's end so light-heartedly, so cheerfully as if it were an operetta? Something is awry if death, madness, delirium, is celebrated as a joyous state relieving us of all pain and cares. She sings as if she drank one glass of champagne too many; but this is the way Donizetti wanted it — the voice of an innocent child, chaste and radical, fragile and bizarre. In this cabaletta the humiliated woman driven to despair finally triumphs over the cruel world of men — like a butterfly fluttering in the air before it disappears. What "mad" ornamentation she wove into the melody in the repeats — her effort to alleviate the fear, to prepare her departure from this oppressive world. Callas alone was capable of adding embellishments that contributed to the dramaturgical and psychological understanding of the situation, an essential extra that crystallizes, personalizes, the mental state of the figure, as if the composed musical phrase were no longer sufficient to capture the explosive power of the figure's emotions.

And how masterfully she interpolates and subtly marks the ornamentation as a kind of subtext in parentheses — her individual interpretation of the main musical phrase. She thus gives us a short lesson in the venerable tradition of bel canto singing, which, in fact, does not tolerate whimsical embellishment, but is based on a strict set of prescribed figures governed by the *haute école* of musical taste. Although the coloratura is imposed upon her by the rules of bel canto, they are individual interpolations, prompted by the heart. And how elegantly she scatters these masterful gems, these diamonds and emeralds, *en passant* as if they were a trifling. Her playful embellishments intensify the coquette cheerfulness of the music, culminating, in the famous measures 14 and 15 of the repeat of the cabaletta, in an eruption, a crossover: the aesthetics of opera, of the closed stage, of the old bel canto tradition is magically dissolved for a few seconds by a minute interpolation. Callas sings the G flat at "pregherò" as written and then proceeds an octave higher from G and A to the final note B flat at the end, where she dares to tie this high B flat to the high C flat of the next phrase before returning to the C flat an octave lower of Donizetti's original notation.

Musical rationalists may see this as a simple trick and dismiss it as a vocal showpiece of high notes. For these people the step-by-step upward movement to "heaven" in the bass of the B flat minor prelude from the first volume of *Das Wohltemperierte Klavier* is merely a game of counterpoint without any deeper meaning. With her four interpolated tones Callas created something similar. She illuminates the emotional power of the text — the unbelievable yearning for her loved one — by extending heaven's ladder a few more steps than the composer planned. And thus the utopia, the fictive other world, is made palpable for one moment. The etheric height of the B flat bathes her thoughts and wishes in a completely different light. Reaching out to heaven, to her bridegroom, takes on a metaphysical coloring that would not have found expression in the earthly regions of the B flat of the original.

Leonora, *Il Trovatora*, lady-in-waiting to the Queen of Aragon.

"The soul of the lady-in-waiting is beautiful because of her chaste promise," Eloi Recoing notes in the program for a Brussels perform-ance in 1984. He must have been thinking of Callas, who with her dark, sensuous, but chaste, tone of untouchable beauty turned her eyes from the horror of the world and per-ceived the message of her beloved only by the inner ear of her heart: "Her love is not of this evil world; her chastity is not humiliation through disappointment, but rather the purifi-cation of desire."

No man is to win her, not if she cannot love him. Even Luna, the cruel warrior of the night, fails although he passionately desires her and is prepared to let the world go up in flames and everyone die, even his own brother. She, the strong, chaste woman, would rather die than give herself to a mad-man. This story is more than the sheltered upper-class girl's dream of the knight in shin-ing armor who will awaken sleeping beauty. "The purity of feeling is achieved in the exalta-tion of the beloved," and as Recoing concludes "it is an absolute love, emblematic from begin-ning to end, a love that yearns for death, its marriage with eternity."

Callas sang this role twenty times on stage between 1950 and 1955. In 1953 alone, her most successful year, she appeared as Leonora twelve times. The most beautiful and intense recording was the Milan studio production in August 1956 under Herbert von Karajan, who had a wonderful feeling for her inner tempi. She was the personification of the nocturnal butterfly that Verdi imagined, with the heart of a lion (Leonora!), the pride of a princess,

the sensuality and the warmth of a Mediterra-nean goddess of love.

"At the tournament. That is where I saw him," she confides to her friend Ines, "dark was his garment and the helmet, dark the shield, without a coat of arms, an unknown warrior who won the laurel wreath." This was her fairy-tale prince who would rescue her. But he disappears again, "like the passing image of a golden dream." And then, on a starry, mild summer night, he suddenly re-appears, singing his melancholy song. Verdi chose the seldom-used, dark key of A flat minor, and Callas's voice takes on a purple-black-brown timbre. Using the most beautiful legato, she moves from these dark regions to the more peaceful fantasy world of A flat major, where absolute, all-encompassing love rules.

"Try to forget him," her confidante Ines tells her gently, sensing the coming tragedy, but there is no hope. Leonora has already given her heart to the troubadour — forever. This certainty restores her spirits and for a few measures she loses herself in a girlish light-heartedness. And then she flutters out into the darkness, singing of love and death, this beautiful creature of the night, in her playful cabaletta in A flat major, which Verdi composed with such a light, floating rhythm as if she were a butterfly or a little bird, sing-ing a love song. Here the nocturnal idyll with its magical purple-colored A flat major is mixed with the chirping of the bird, and the singer must be able to express this contrast between the dark smoldering of the soul and the feathery lightness of the bird's colora-tura.

The text has lost its importance here; it is overpowered by Verdi's fantastic music, the stylized song of the nightingale with its craggy melodic phrase. This is Leonora's teas-ingly playful, but bitterly earnest, answer to the sad and tantalizing song of the Troubadour. And only Callas was able to capture both elements in her voice: child-like chirping and feminine sensuality, bright and dark, light and heavy, girl and woman, chastity and eroticism, passion and sprightly elegance. This is not the overflowing fantasy of a teenage girl in love, it is the vow of loyalty spoken with the intense feeling of a woman who holds her word: "S'io non vivró per esso, per esso moriró!" If I cannot live for him, I will die for him.

Norma, high priestess of the druids, *Casta Diva*.

Between 1948 and 1965 Callas appeared eighty-nine times on stage as Bellini's high priestess of the druids, in twenty-six productions and under ten conductors. She thus chose Bellini's tragic and heroic role as her favorite, her life's role. This preference was based on the music, for Bellini's (and Donizetti's) early Romantic, puristic bel canto — untouched by realism — was at the heart of Callas's sublime, inner-directed art.

There are also numerous parallels to her own life. Callas herself was unable to escape her role as a priestess of art, and she had to pay for this privilege with her own private happiness. Was the fairy tale a sanctuary for her soul? As a childless heroine of the twentieth century, Callas had to give up more than her sisters of antiquity, before the higher powers reclaimed her voice and relieved her of her duties. As an artist she was — even more than in the antique roles she played — a *casta diva*, a radical and single-minded priestess of absolute art, a "blind" visionary with magical powers, the fire-spewing medium of the primal forces of the universe.

Casta diva: Act 1. Stage directions: "With the sickle, Norma cuts the mistletoe. The priestesses gather it up in woven baskets. Norma comes forward, lifting her arms toward the heavens, where the moon is shining clear and bright. All prostrate themselves as she sings her prayer."

Norma: Chaste goddess, who dost bathe in
    silver light
    These ancient, hallowed trees,
    Turn thy fair face upon us,
    Unveiled and unclouded...

    Temper, o goddess,
    Temper the burning hearts,
    The excessive zeal of thy people.
    Enfold the earth in that sweet peace
    Which through thee, reigns in
    heaven.

Callas alone was able to capture in her voice this nocturnal, magical atmosphere, this holy silence of the divine spheres, this landscape bathed in the moon's silvery beams. Perhaps her most beautiful performance was the Roman RAI production of 1955 under Tullio Serafin, a performance in which for once the choir was fairly professional. It is not important which of her six stage, three studio, or half-dozen concert recordings one listens to, for she was always beyond reach of her competitors. The most lyrical, most moving, interpretation of this aria was in November 1949, recorded during a series of rehearsals under Arturo Basile with a miserable orchestra, without a choir and without Oroveso. Callas sings like an angel, in the most beautiful piano, with sheer inexhaustible breath control. No other singer has transformed the wonderful A at the beginning of this *preghiera* into such an intense, warm, glowing sound. Her voice is like the barely visible, gentle flickering of a candle. Her vibrato is slow, one can feel the quiet beat of its pulse; it is stimulating as well as soothing, and it resounds gently in our souls. And how wonderfully she spans Bellini's unending melodic phrases, gradually building up the irregular line of the phrase until it finally reaches its climax.

And when, to emphasize her request for peace, she sings a high F at the end of the second verse, shortly before the dizzy descent of the glissando cadence, she puts her entire soul and art into this one tone. In this *messo di voce*, the last monumental grace note before the dominant, she encapsulates — over a foreboding harmony — all the cathartic powers of music and its divine message. Once again time stood still, a moment was transformed, her feminine creative powers abolished the mechanical laws of time.

Callas's sense of timing was absolutely archaic, of classical Greek origin, and fed by a primordial, matriarchal instinct diametrically opposed to the merciless, chronometric pace of the capitalistic, male-dominated society of the twentieth century. The meter was only a vessel, a framework, an idea for the movement, which she filled freely with her creative energy. Her use of *tempo rubato* corresponded to her sense of time, the measured time of Greek antiquity and its heroes, whose individual drama of destiny determined the movement of time, not some anonymous power. This is why it is senseless to accuse her of dragging the tempi as do those meticulous fanatics who see the voice only as a soulless instrument. For Callas, choice and modification of tempo were always inextricably connected with the emotional coloring of the tone. The meaning, the emotional content, and expressive value of a musical phrase determine the tempo, and the numerous, little delays, every individual tone, even the most minute ornamentation were aesthetically refined, filled with emotion, with meaning, released from the strict meter, endowed with a special aura, and given a palpable form. And thus in all of her musical creations she left to posterity not only antique statues of inimitable beauty and of solid consistency but also the personified epitomes of female greatness, passion, fortitude, and beauty.

She rescued opera from near oblivion, imbued the ancient heroines with their archaic power, with their frightening will to shape destiny, with their siren song, and rekindled the exhausted inner powers of mankind with their glowing invocations and their moving pleas.

"Who could have resisted her voice?" Yves Saint-Laurent asks in his obituary, which he concludes by confessing: "I fell in love with her." He mourns her death, but is convinced that her spirit and her message live on. And my response is: I am in love — with all the women she created and immortalized. In love with her invisible demon whose identity was only manifest in her voice, but which continually changed both in her operatic roles and in her life. This demon is alive, recorded in innumerable documents, preserved and protected in the imaginary record museum. And any one who is so inclined can listen and be enchanted, moved, overwhelmed, by its humanizing powers — powers that to this day have not lost one iota of their vehemence, their magic, and cathartic effect. Even though we cannot see Callas with our own eyes, we feel her overpowering presence all the more.

Photographs of Callas, on the other hand, seem almost historic: they document a past era — the post-war fifties and sixties before the pop revolution. One can detect the attempt of the great photographers to reveal her invisible aura, but the numerous transformations of her appearance are themselves expressions of an inner demon, they make up the mortal frame the messenger of the gods had to assume in order to exist; in retrospect they appear to be additional roles that she played in order to provide a modicum of protection for her inner self. She shared the destiny of many angels that took on human form and possessed the powers to transform it as they pleased.

Strange indeed were those who sought her proximity and discouraged her from fulfilling her mission in life — those unsavory creatures who almost always follow in the paths of prophets and saviors. For the holy, pure, and illuminated is often attracted to shadowy figures and at their mercy. Some of the private photographs of Callas demonstrate the helplessness of the heroine, who after leaving the stage of history, the heroic site of her struggle, stumbles into the depths of mundane life. Nevertheless, the longer one studies the photos of Callas, the less comprehensible her talent, her artistic beauty, her inner strength, her musicality appear.

"And suddenly from the background came a blazing voice, heavy, sharp, piercing — wonderful and out of this world — an incomparable voice made to conquer death. It was a magical voice, that of a genius, with all its oddities and all its faults. The syncopation and marvellous high notes that took our breath, the trills, the vocalization, intensity and shrillness that erupted in bolts of lightning … It is the voice of the courageous Siren who bridles the waves of the ocean and draws them to the rocks of her modulations where they break.

Diva of all divas, empress, queen, goddess, witch, sorceress. Divine and sublime. Devastator, fugitive, nightingale, turtle dove. She traveled through this century like a great, lonely eagle whose soaring flight forever protects us — we who have outlived her." (Yves Saint-Laurent)

And Tito Gobbi, her stage partner of many years, once said "I always believed that she was immortal and she is!"

George and Evangelia Kalogeropoulos with their two daughters, Maria (b. 1923)
and Jackie (b. 1917), in New York, 1924.

New York, 1934. Ten-year-old Maria (front left) with family and relatives: her father (far left), her mother Evangelia (back row, second from the right), her sister Jackie (front right). In the same year Maria gave her first public appearance at a talent show sponsored by WOR, a New York radio station. Accompanied by her sister, she sang Yradier's "La Paloma" and a film song, "A Heart That Is Free," winning second prize, a Bulova watch.

Maria Kalogeropoulos (left) with other voice students of Elvira de Hidalgo, bathing after a successful performance of Suor Angelica *at the Odeon Concert Hall in Athens on June 16, 1940.*

Private photograph taken during the war in Athens, ca. 1940.

*Maria Callas with her teacher Louise Caselotti on the freighter S.S. "Rossia" on the way
from New York to Naples in June 1947. Louise Caselotti was the wife of New York lawyer and opera
impresario Eddie Bagaroczy, who had just arranged an "exclusive" ten-year contract with
Callas, granting him ten percent of her entire income. Six months previously, in January 1947, Bagaroczy's
business venture failed: a private opera company in a production of Puccini's* Turandot *in Chicago with
Callas in the title role.*

Three days after her arrival in Italy, Maria Callas met the owner of a brick factory,
Giovanni Battista Meneghini. "On August 1 [1947] I accompanied her on an excursion to Venice and we fell
in love," wrote Meneghini in his book on the famous singer. Callas gave this photograph to
her admirer. They were married on April 21, 1949, in Verona.

Maria Callas as Violetta in Mexico City, 1951/52. She starred in Verdi's opera La Traviata
four times in July 1951 at the Palacio de las Bellas Artes in Mexico City.
In these performances she laid the foundation for her unrivaled dramatic interpretation of this role.

Maria Callas at an official photo session in 1952.

Maria Callas in the production of La Traviata *at the Teatro la Fenice in Venice, January 1952, where she sang twice (on January 8 and 10). At the time she weighed more than 190 pounds.*

Maria Callas with her husband Giovanni Battista Meneghini at the airport in Mexico City after their
first transatlantic flight together, June 1951.

Callas trying on her costume for the title role in Ponchielli's opera La Gioconda, *her second Scala premiere.*
After opening the new Milan season with her incomparable interpretation of Lady Macbeth just three
weeks previously, she celebrated her second triumph as Ponchielli's street singer in December 1952.
She was now Italy's prima donna assoluta.

Maria Callas as Marguerite in Act III of Arrigo Boito's Faust setting, Mefistofele.
She sang this role only three times at the Roman Arena in Verona, July 1954.
In this year she had lost over sixty pounds.

Maria Callas as Lucia di Lammermoor in her dressing room at La Scala, January 1954. The new production, conducted and directed by Herbert von Karajan, became one of the outstanding achievements in Callas's triumphant career. The Scala Company gave guest performances of this production in Berlin (1955) and in Vienna (1956) to enraptured audiences.

Right: Portrait of the emerging world star as she began slimming in 1953.
Photograph by John Deakin.

Maria Callas as Lucia di Lammermoor in the Mad Scene of Act II at La Scala in 1954. Her performance of Donizetti's tragic heroine became a milestone of operatic history. The uniqueness of her musical interpretation is still evident in the live recording of the Scala Company's guest performance in Berlin, autumn 1955. Photograph by Erio Piccagliani.

Page 54

Maria Callas as Elisabeth de Valois in the Scala production of Verdi's Don Carlo, April 1954. Although she sang this role only five times, all of which under Antonino Votto, her dramatic performance was to set new standards. After 1958 she continued to give recital performances of Elisabeth's famous aria, "Tu che la vanita," and sometimes Princess Eboli's, "O don fatale."

Page 55

An unusual snapshot by Erio Piccagliani, a veteran photographer at La Scala, taken from the right side of the stage during the final scene of Gluck's opera Alceste, which Maria Callas sang four times in April 1954 under Carlo Maria Giulini in Margherita Wallmann's production.

Recording Ruggero Leoncavallo's opera I Pagliacci, *June 12–17, 1954, in Milan. From left to right: Giuseppe di Stefano (Canio), Maria Callas (Nedda), Rolando Panerai (Silvio), Tito Gobbi (Tonio), Nicola Monti (Beppe), and conductor Tullio Serafin. Although she never sang Nedda on stage, her recording set new standards for this role.*

Right: Portrait of thirty-year-old Maria Callas, probably taken during her stay in London, September 1954. Photograph by Angus McBean.

Anonymous portrait of Maria Callas, aged thirty, Milan 1954.

Maria Callas in the title role of Vincenzo Bellini's Norma shortly before her U.S. debut on November 1,
1954, at the Civic Opera House in Chicago.
She gave two performances under Nicola Rescigno to wildly enthusiastic audiences.

*Luchino Visconti, the most important stage director to work with Callas, at a rehearsal of the
new production of Gasparo Spontini's* La Vestale, *which opened her third season in a row at La Scala.
She sang the role in this production only, in a series of five performances.
Photograph by Erio Piccagliani.*

Right: Maria Callas with her hair dyed blond at a rehearsal of the Milan production of La Vestale *in 1954.
Photograph by Erio Piccagliani.*

At a rehearsal of La Vestale *in Milan, 1954. Photograph by Erio Piccagliani.*

Right: Maria Callas as Giulia in the new production of La Vestale *at* La Scala, *December 1954.*
It was Visconti's first opera and the Scala debut of tenor Franco Corelli, who sang the role of the
Roman captain Licinio.
Photograph by Erio Piccagliani.

Maria Callas as Giulia in the Scala production of December 1954. Luchino Visconti praised her "intensity, expression, everything . . . ." Photograph by Erio Piccagliani.

Pages 66–67

Maria Callas, tenor Cesare Valletti, director Luchino Visconti, and conductor Leonard Bernstein discussing a new production of Bellini's opera La Sonnambula, *which premiered at La Scala on March 5, 1955. In December 1953, she had performed Cherubini's* Médée *in Milan with Bernstein conducting. He later called her the "world's greatest artist."*

Maria Callas as the sleepwalking Swiss village girl Amina in Bellini's melodrama La Sonnambula,
a Visconti production at La Scala in 1955. She sang this, her most illustrious, role sixteen times at
La Scala and six times in guest performances with the Scala Company in Cologne and Edinburgh.
The recording of her performance in Cologne, July 1957, is a highlight of opera history.
Photograph by Erio Piccagliani.

Pages 70–71

Maria Callas as Violetta (left: letter scene, Act II; right: banquet scene, picture II, Act II) in
Visconti's second Scala production, which experts still regard as the most beautiful, moving production of
Verdi's La Traviata in this century and as Callas's most outstanding acting performance.
Between 1951 and 1958 she sang this role sixty-three times.
Photograph by Erio Piccagliani.

Maria Callas in Milan, ca. 1955.

Page 74

Publicity still for the recording of Puccini's
Madame Butterfly, produced in August
1955 in Milan under Herbert von Karajan.

Page 75

The most famous of Callas's press photos.
It established her reputation worldwide as the
"Greek fury." If anyone had behaved
scandalously, however, it was
U.S. Marshal Stanley Pringle (foreground).
Immediately after her third performance of
Madame Butterfly at the Chicago Lyric Opera
on November 17, 1955, Pringle brought
to the prima donna's dressing room
the papers accusing her of withholding royalty
fee payments from her manager
Eddie Bagaroczy and stuck the indictment
in her costume. The diva's response
was unequivocal, and the photo reporter from
the Associated Press got the snapshot
of his life. As early as 1960 Callas's
biographer George Jellinek wondered whether
the incident was a maneuver by the Chicago
anti-Callas fraction to damage her reputation.

Portrait of the 32-year-old diva in 1956. Photograph by David Seymour.

Right: Maria Callas shortly before an afternoon stroll with her industrious husband and
agent Giovanni Battista Meneghini.
Photograph by David Seymour, Rome 1956.

Pages 84–85

The prima donna at her daily practice session. Photograph by David Seymour, Rome 1956.

Maria Callas as guest star at the opening gala of the International Film Festival in Venice,
August 28, 1956.

Pages 88–89

Maria Callas and her husband on holiday at Lake Garda, summer 1955.
Callas was thirty-one and Meneghini fifty-eight years old.

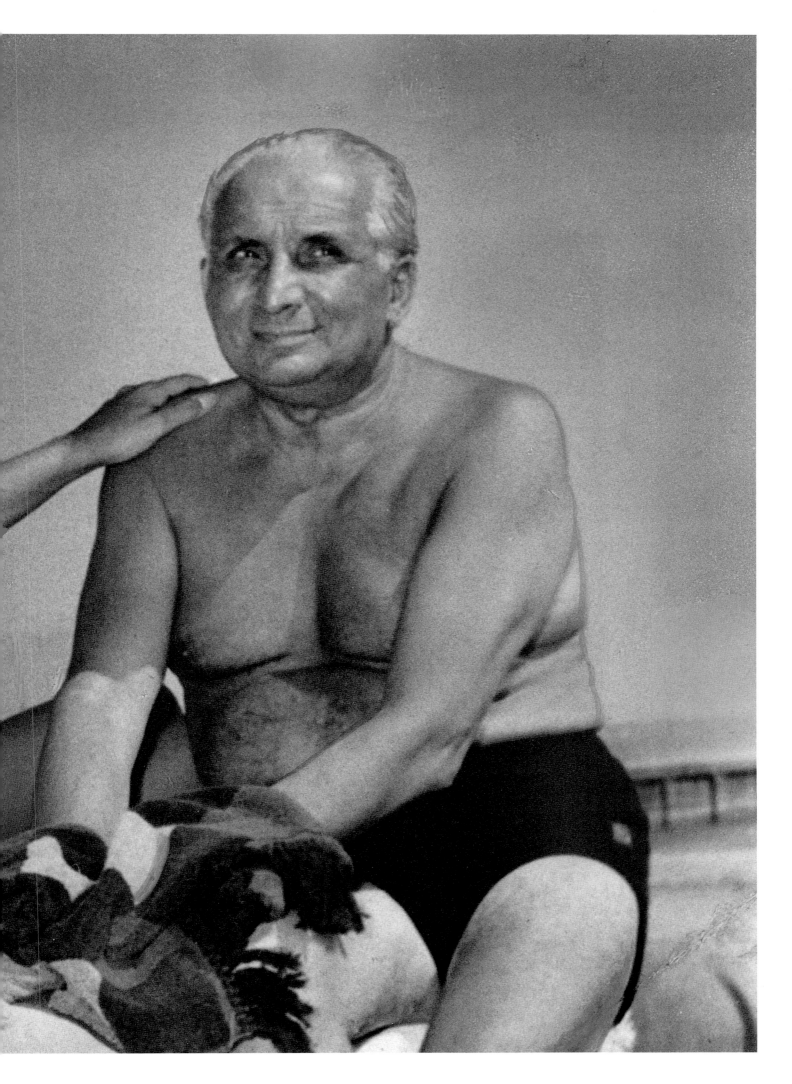

Maria Callas and Herbert von Karajan during a rehearsal of a guest performance of
Lucia di Lammermoor *at the Metropolitan Opera House, December 3, 1956. Like Bernstein,*
Karajan was one of her most fervent admirers.
Photograph by Erio Piccagliani.

Right: A curtain call after Callas's first performance of Lucia di Lammermoor *at the Metropolitan Opera*
House on December 3, 1956. It was her thirty-third birthday. Elsa Maxwell wrote in her critique:
"I confess the great Callas acting in the Mad Scene left me completely unmoved . . . ." In the same month
Callas succeeded in winning the affection of the feared gossip columnist.

Maria Callas with her poodle "Toy" arriving in New York from Chicago on January 23, 1957, where her concert at the Civic Opera received enthusiastic acclaim.

92

May 7, 1957: Maria Callas greeting her new friend Elsa Maxwell at the Milan airport. The prima donna was rehearsing, under Visconti's direction, a new production of Gluck's opera Iphigénie en Tauride, *the premiere of which was scheduled for June 1.*

Maria Callas in Visconti's production of Donizetti's seldom performed opera Anna Bolena,
which she sang twelve times in two seasons at La Scala beginning in April 1957.

Elsa Maxwell at a dress rehearsal of Gluck's Iphigénie en Tauride *in Callas's dressing room
at La Scala, May 1957.*

*Right: Maria Callas as Iphigenia before her dressing room mirror. The Gluck opera was her twentieth
production at La Scala and her fifth and last collaboration with Visconti. Photograph by Willy Rizzo.*

Publicity shot for a recording of Puccini's Turandot in July 1957 with the Scala Company under Tullio Serafin. Her final stage performance of this opera was in 1949.

Maria Callas posing in a bathing suit on the Lido in Venice, summer 1957.

Early September 1957: Maria Callas and shipping magnate Aristoteles Onassis at an afternoon cocktail party at the Excelsior Hotel in Venice, to which Duchess Natalia Volpi had invited the Meneghinis, Elsa Maxwell, and Aristoteles Onassis.

Pages 102–3

September 3, 1957: At the Venice Film Festival, Elsa Maxwell hosts a luxurious costume ball in honor of her "dear friend" Maria Callas. One hundred fifty guests, including numerous film stars and Aristoteles Onassis, cavorted in mostly lavish historical costumes. From left to right: Elsa Maxwell with a genuine doge cap from the fourteenth century, next to her Princess Ruspoli masquerading as a cat, and Maria Callas. The singer and the shipping magnate are supposed to have become better acquainted at this party.

Portrait of Maria Callas, aged thirty-three, taken by Cecil Beaton, London 1957.

Maria Callas as Amelia in La Scala's new production of Verdi's Un ballo in maschera *on December 7,*
1957, her sixth season-opening premiere in Milan. She sang this role five times on stage, achieving an unrivaled
performance. Photography by Erio Piccagliani.

Right: The prima donna after her triumphant performance of Un ballo in maschera *at La Scala,*
December 7, 1957. Behind her is Ettore Bastianini, who sang the part of the conspirator Renato
and on the left, next to the guard, conductor Gianandrea Gavazzeni.

The gala performance of Bellini's Norma *in Rome on January 2, 1958, led to the greatest scandal of the singer's career. Because of a sore throat Callas refused to continue the performance after Act I, leading to adverse headlines throughout the world. Public anger was at its height in Italy, and the tabloid press called her the moodiest prima donna of all times. This day marked the turning point of her career, especially since her voice was beginning to weaken.*
Photograph by John Dominis.

Callas leaving the stage after her decision not to sing Act II of Norma.

*Right: The audience in heated discussion after Callas's walk-out on January 2, 1958, in Rome.
In the royal loge: Italian's premier Gronchi, who complained that he was not informed in
good time of the prima donna's decision.*

The prima donna, who was bitterly attacked from all sides, receives support from Luchino Visconti in her Rome hotel.

112

January 7, 1958: Callas holding an international press conference at the Hotel Quirinale in Rome.
She refutes all the accusations brought against her and disarms the reporters with her wit, charm,
and command of the situation.

Milan, January 16, 1958: the Meneghinis with "Toy," boarding their flight to the U.S.

Right: Paris, January 16, 1958. Maria Callas in front of her own picture at the Hotel Crillon before attending a gala dinner in her honor sponsored by the French EMI.

*The gala dinner at Maxim's where Callas spent exactly eighty-four minutes
(of her six-hour stopover in Paris). Photograph by Garofalo.*

Horst P. Horst photographed Maria Callas during her stay in New York, spring 1958.

*Rudolf Bing, the powerful superintendent of the Metropolitan Opera House,
congratulating Callas after her magnificent performance of* La Traviata *on February 6, 1958.
In the background a skeptical Meneghini.*

Right: Ten curtain calls for her performance of La Traviata *at the Met, February 6, 1958. Four weeks later
she sang for the last time in the city of her birth and at an
opera house she never particularly liked.*

*Maria Callas as Imogene in Bellini's Il Pirata, her last important performance in Milan, photographed by
Erio Piccagliani. Weary of the intrigues and Superintendent Ghiringhelli's continual disdain,
Callas took leave of the Scala, which for seven years she had made the focal point of the opera world,
on May 31, 1958 after the fifth performance of Il Pirata and 157 other appearances there.
At her farewell the audience awarded her an endless ovation, which Ghiringhelli brought to a close by
letting down the heavy safety curtain. Right: Callas leaving the theater, surrounded by her fans.
Ghiringhelli scoffed: "Prima donnas come and prima donnas go, but La Scala remains."*

Maria Callas in La Traviata *at Covent Garden, June 1958. Photograph by Houston Rogers.*

Between June 20 and 30, 1958, Callas sang her last five European performances of La Traviata *at Covent Garden. Two final appearances of her quintessential role followed in Dallas in October.*

Maria Callas as Medea in the production of the Dallas Civic Opera, November 1958.
She sang Cherubini's Médée *twice in Dallas and thirty-one times at other opera houses.*
Photographs by Derek Halstead.

Page 130

Callas as Medea in Dallas, November 1958. Photograph by Derek Halstead.

Page 131

On November 6, 1958, the day of her performance in Dallas, New York's opera director
Rudolf Bing announced the cancellation of her contract with the Metropolitan Opera House.
At a press conference in Dallas, which Elsa Maxwell also attended, Callas countered that she had no
desire to sing the same roles over and over – Violetta in La Traviata,
Tosca or Lady Macbeth – the parts offered her by Bing.

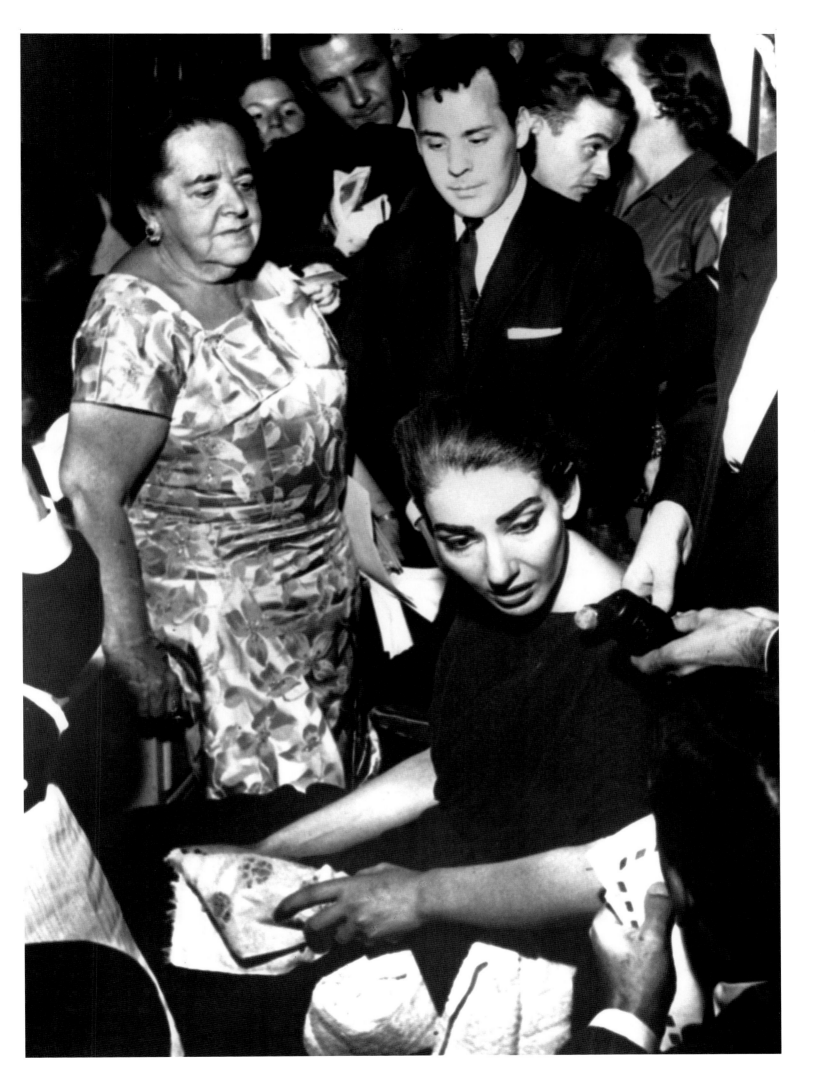

Callas and Meneghini in their hotel, a few hours before her Parisian recital debut at the Palais Garnier, December 19, 1958. Photograph by Claude Azoulay.

Right: Callas with her poodle in a bar during a short stay in Paris, October 1958.

Callas's Parisian debut on December 19, 1958, at the opera house. Her program was a strange mixture,
beginning with three arias from Norma, Il travatore, *and* Il barbiere di Siviglia.
After the intermission there followed a scenic presentation of Act II from Puccini's Tosca.
The concert was a benefit for the French League of Honor. The entire Parisian elite – Chaplin,
Brigitte Bardot, Jean Cocteau, Françoise Sagan, and Aristoteles Onassis – were present.
The concert was broadcast live in all Western European countries.
Photographs by Jean-Pierre Leloir.

France's president Coty greeting Callas at her gala concert on December 19, 1958.

Right: The gala dinner for 450 guests, including Aristoteles Onassis.
Photograph by François Gragnon.

Maria Callas in Paris the day after her triumphant recital debut.
Photograph by François Gragnon.

Right: Portrait photo of the 35-year-old prima donna taken by Zoe Dominic during
her stay in London in 1959.

Callas landing in New York to give a concert performance of Bellini's opera Il Pirata *at Carnegie Hall. Her contract with the Met had been cancelled on November 6, 1958.*

Right: In Philadelphia under Eugene Ormandy, Maria Callas gives a recital of arias from Mefistofele, Il barbiere di Siviglia, *and* Hamlet.

Maria Callas at a rehearsal of Médée *in London, 1959. Photograph by Douglas Glass.*

Pages 144–45

In June 1959 Callas sings Médée five times under Nicola Rescigno. In addition to four performances in Dallas in November, these are her only stage appearances this year.

Two scenes from the beginning of Act II of the 1959 Médée production in London.
Photographs by Houston Rogers.

Aristoteles Onassis and Maria Callas after the premiere of Médée *at a midnight party in her honor at the Dorchester Hotel in London, June 17, 1959.*

Callas leaving the Dorchester at 3:00 A.M., June 18, 1959. Photograph by Desmond O'Neill.

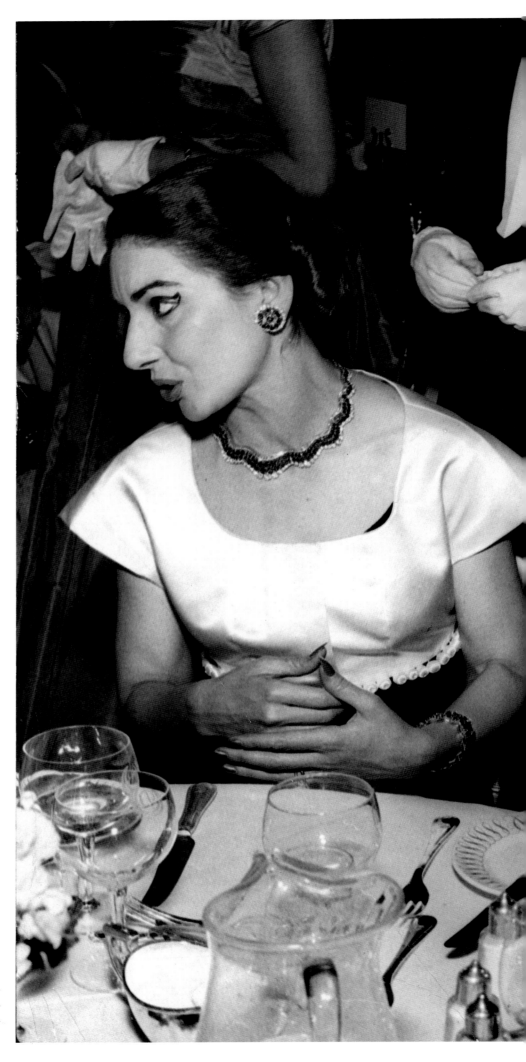

Maria Callas, Onassis, and Randolph Churchill, the son of Winston Churchill, at the midnight party at the Dorchester Hotel celebrating her London premiere of Médée. Photograph by Desmond O'Neill.

July 22, 1959: Callas boarding the luxury yacht "Christina" for a three-week Mediterranean cruise, to which the Meneghinis had been invited by Onassis in London. With them are Sir Winston Churchill and his wife, Fiat chief executive Agnelli and his wife, Onassis's wife Christina and her sister. During the cruise Callas tells her husband that she has fallen in love with Onassis and wants a separation. Photographs by Edward Quinn.

Sir Winston Churchill aboard the "Christina."

Maria Callas in conversation with Sir Winston aboard the "Christina." Photographs by Edward Quinn.

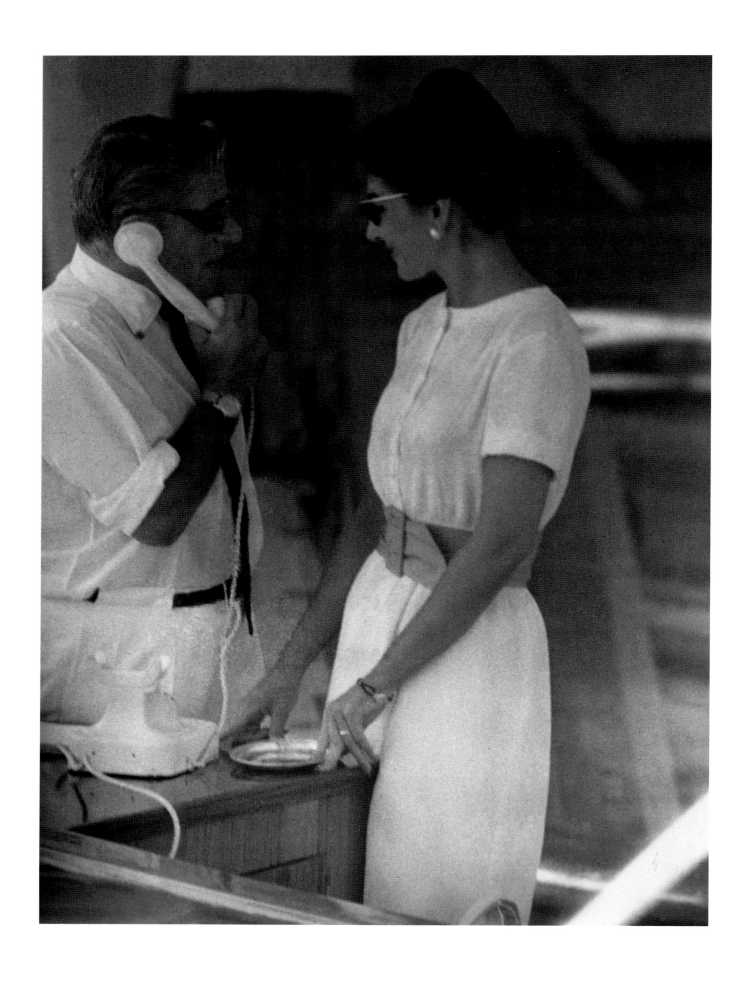

The shipping magnate and the opera diva on the luxury yacht.

From left to right: Tina Onassis, Maria Callas, a grim Meneghini, and Sir Winston Churchill on the "Christina." Photograph by Edward Quinn.

An evening at the theater in Monaco during the cruise. Left: Tina Onassis, Maria Callas, and Lady Churchill. Right: Churchill and Onassis.

During the Mediterranean cruise on the "Christina": Maria Callas and Tina Onassis in Delphi.

Pages 162–63

Maria Callas and Onassis in the amphitheater in Delphi.

Night life on the "Christina." Front right: Meneghini holding a cigarette, to his left an exuberant Callas, and Onassis on the far left.

Lovers of the year: Onassis and Callas aboard the "Christina" before Capri.

Maria Callas in Milan, fleeing reporters, September 7, 1959.

Onassis trying to hide his identity on the way from the Milan airport to Callas's apartment in the Via Buonarotti, September 7, 1959.

Before flying to London for a recital, Maria Callas enjoys a short stay on the "Christina" at the harbor in Rome, September 22, 1959.

Right: Callas's first concert at the Royal Festival Hall, September 23, 1959. The audience's ovation lasted twelve minutes and a reporter commented that "the tiger" appeared very relaxed.

Shopping with her poodle "Toy" in Milan, October 1, 1959.

On her way to Nice on October 3, 1959, after a television appearance in London, Callas is chauffeured to her plane at the Paris airport to avoid reporters. Obviously, she did not manage to escape them all.

November 14, 1959: Giovanni Battista Meneghini and his lawyer approaching the courthouse in Brescia.
After a six-hour hearing, Judge Cesare Andreotti decreed a separation by "mutual consent."
Meneghini retained the villa in Sirmione; Callas kept her jewelry and the Milan apartment.

Right: Maria Callas and her lawyer leaving the courthouse in Brescia, November 14, 1959.
A day before the settlement, she was informed that in the coming season she was not scheduled
to sing at La Scala.
The title roles had been given to Renata Tebaldi, her greatest rival.

Maria Callas at her dressing table before her appearance in Médée at the Dallas Civic Opera.
After this triumph on November 21, 1959, there followed a sabbatical of more than a year,
interrupted only by two performances of Norma at the Epidauros theater in August 1960.

The lonely diva in Paris, 1960. Photograph by Dalmas.

Left: Maria Callas during her second London recital at St. James's Palace on May 30, 1961.
It was her only concert appearance that year. Photograph by Houston Rogers.

February 1960: Twenty months after her break with La Scala, Maria Callas attends a film premiere in Milan
with Superintendent Antonio Ghiringhelli, immediately causing speculation that
Callas will return to La Scala.

September 9, 1960: Callas and Onassis cause a sensation by attending the International Sporting Club ball in Monte Carlo. Photograph by Edward Quinn.

Maria Callas and Luchino Visconti at a restaurant in Milan, November 1960.
Visconti was originally contracted as stage director for the new production of Donizetti's Poliuto at La Scala,
but he cancelled after the Italian censors objected to his film Rocco and his Brothers.
The German director Herbert Graf took over the production.

Pages 180–81

On July 24 and 28, Callas appeared in two performances of Bellini's Norma in the antique theater of
Epidauros. It was her first performance in Greece in fifteen years.

Page 183

Maria Callas as Paolina in Donizetti's opera Poliuto, the next to the last Scala production of her career,
December 1960. H.C. Robbins Landon wrote in High Fidelity, "Callas is not what she once was,"
and Harold R. Rosenthal spoke of "Callas imitating Callas." Photograph by Erio Piccagliani.

Callas as Paolina in the Scala production of Poliuto, *December 1960.*

Right: Final applause after the premiere of Poliuto *on December 7, 1960.*
The title role was sung by Franco Corelli.

Applause for Callas's not entirely successful comeback at La Scala. In the top loge on the left, the Begum Aga Kahn, below right, Onassis and Prince Rainier of Monaco.

Maria Callas and Aristoteles Onassis arriving at the New Year's Eve ball at the
Sporting Club of Monte Carlo.

The diva and the shipping magnate at the New Year's Eve ball in Monte Carlo, 1961.

The "scandalous" couple, strolling at night along the yacht harbor of Monte Carlo, where they thought they would be safe from curious onlookers.

Onassis and Callas on November 14, 1961, walking on Brook Street after dinner at Claridge's in London.

197

March 12, 1962: Callas at the Kongreßsaal of the Deutsches Museum in Munich – the first recital during a ten-day tour of Germany which takes her to Hamburg, Essen, and Bonn. Under Georges Prêtre she sings arias from operas by Rossini, Verdi, Massenet, and Bizet, including a moving interpretation of Princess Eboli's aria from Don Carlo. Right: A carnation after her Munich recital; above: a rose in Hamburg.

Callas at the Hotel Ritz in Paris in the early 1960s. Since 1961 permanently in Paris, she first lived on Avenue Foch, no. 44. In 1967 she moved to a luxurious apartment on Avenue Georges-Mandel, no. 36, where she remained until her death on September 16, 1977. Photograph by Garofalo.

Publicity still for a Carmen *recording conducted by Georges Prêtre, 1964.*

Callas as Tosca at her London comeback, January 1964. Until February 5 she appeared at Covent Garden in seven wildly acclaimed performances.

In 1965 Callas appeared as Puccini's tragic heroine Tosca nine times in Paris (right: Act II with Tito Gobbi as Scarpia), two times at the Metropolitan Opera House (above), and in her last opera performance at Covent Garden on July 5, 1965.

At her Paris comeback in July 1964, Callas sang, in addition to Tosca, the second most frequent title role in her career – Norma in Franco Zeffirelli's production. She appeared on stage most often in this role: eighty-nine times. In May and June 1964 she performed Norma eight times in Paris and in the following year five times. Although her voice was clearly declining and wobbly in the high range, critics agreed that she "was able to get more out of this role than any other singer" (H. Rosenthal). Photograph by Eliot Elisofon.

The diva and the new film stars: Maria Callas with Alain Delon at a gala in Paris, 1968.

Summit of the stars: Maria Callas, Liz Taylor, and Onassis at a benefit gala in 1964.

*A moving farewell after her last opera performance in
Tosca at Covent Garden, July 5, 1965.
Photograph by Maurice Sayers.*

The prima donna assoluta *and the stars of the pop generation: Sylvie Vartan and Johnny Halliday at a gala dinner celebrating the reopening of the Lido in Paris, 1966. Photograph by Dalmas.*

Left: Paris nightlife: Maria Callas dancing with Roland Petit.

Maria Callas and Onassis at a late hour, enjoying the gala at the Lido, 1966.

Callas on her last cruise with Onassis, in Nassau, Bahamas, summer 1967.

With Onassis in London, shortly before his marriage to Jackie Kennedy.

A photo portrait of Maria Callas, aged forty-five, by Christian Steiner.

Callas dancing with Omar Sharif in Paris, 1969.

225

Maria Callas starring in Medea, *a film of the Euripides tragedy by Pier Paolo Pasolini.
Photograph by Mario Tursi.*

Pages 228–29

Pasolini and Callas during the filming of Medea, *1969. Photograph by Mario Tursi.*

Maria Callas in Pasolini's Medea. *Photograph by Mario Tursi.*

Ninth recital of Callas's world farewell tour at the Théâtre des Champs-Elysées on December 8, 1973.
Photograph by Gérard Neuvecelles.

Pages 234–35

The ecstatic audience after her farewell recital in Paris, December 8, 1973.

Photo portrait of Maria Callas in the early 1970s.

Maria Callas died on September 16, 1977, in Paris. The funeral took place on September 20 in the
Greek Orthodox Church on Rue Georges Bizet.

Princess Grace Patricia and Princess Caroline of Monaco leading the funeral procession, September 20, 1977.

Appendix

List of Operatic Roles

From 2 April 1939 to 5 July 1965,
Maria Callas appeared in more than six hundred
performances of forty-one
operas and operettas.

Eugène d'Albert
Tiefland — Martha
10 performances (1944−45)

Ludwig van Beethoven
Fidelio — Leonore
9 performances (1944)

Vincenzo Bellini
Il Pirata — Imogene
7 performances (1958−59)
La Sonnambula — Amina
22 performances (1955−57)
Norma
89 performances (1948−65)
I Puritani — Elvira
16 performances (1949−55)

Arrigo Boito
Mefistofele — Margherita
3 performances (1954)

Luigi Cherubini
Medea
31 performances (1953−62)

Gaetano Donizetti
Anna Bolena
12 performances (1957−58)
Lucia di Lammermoor
46 performances (1952−56)
Poliuto — Paolina
5 performances (1960)

Christoph Willibald Gluck
Orfeo ed Euridice
2 performances (1951)
Alceste
4 performances (1954)
Iphigénie en Tauride
4 performances (1957)

Umberto Giordano
Andrea Chénier — Madeleine
6 performances (1955)
Fedora
6 performances (1956)

Manolis Kalomiris
O Protomastoras — Smaragda
17 performances (1943−44)

Pietro Mascagni
Cavalleria Rusticana — Santuzza
13 performances (1939, 1944)

Wolfgang Amadeus Mozart
Die Entführung aus dem Serail — Constanze
4 performances (1952)

Carl Millöcker
Der Bettelstudent — Laura
4 performances (1945)

Amilcare Ponchielli
La Gioconda
13 performances (1947−53)

Giacomo Puccini
Tosca
51 performances (1942−65)
Madama Butterfly
3 performances (1955)
Suor Angelica
1 performance (1940)
Turandot
24 performances (1948−49)

Gioacchino Rossini
Il Turco in Italia — Fiorilla
9 performances (1950, 1955)
Il Barbiere di Siviglia — Rosina
5 performances (1956)
Armida
3 performances (1952)

Gasparo Spontini
La Vestale — Giulia
5 performances (1954)

Franz von Suppé
Boccaccio — Beatrice
about 10 performances (1940−41)

Giuseppe Verdi
Nabucco — Abigaille
3 performances (1949)
Macbeth — Lady Macbeth
5 performances (1952)
Rigoletto — Gilda
2 performances (1952)
Il Trovatore — Leonora
20 performances (1950−55)
La Traviata — Violetta
63 performances (1951−58)
Les Vêpres Siciliennes — Elena
11 performances (1951−52)
Un Ballo in Maschera — Amelia
5 performances (1956)
La Forza del Destino — Leonora
6 performances (1948, 1954)
Don Carlo — Elisabeth
5 performances (1954)
Aida
33 performances (1948−53)

Richard Wagner
Tristan und Isolde — Isolde
12 performances (1947−50)
Die Walküre — Brünhilde
6 performances (1949)
Parsifal — Kundry
5 performances (1949−50)

Chronology of Stage Appearances

◇ indicates the program

1938

11 April **Concert** Athens, Parnassos Hall
The students of Maria Trivella's class at the National Conservatory
Pianist: Stefanos Valetsiotis
◇ Weber: *Der Freischütz*, Agathe's aria, M. Callas — Gonoud: *La Reine de Saba*, "Plus grand dans son obscurité" — Psarouda: Greek song — Puccini: *Tosca*, M. Callas (Tosca) in a duet with J. Kambanis

1939

2 April ***Cavalleria Rusticana*** by Pietro Mascagni Athens, Olympia Theater
M. Callas (Santuzza), V. Semeriotis (Turiddu), A. Kopanu (Lucia), C. Athenseos (Alfio), P. Euthemiadu (Lola)

22 May **Concert** Athens, Parnassos Hall
The students of Maria Trivella's class at the National Conservatory
Pianist: Stefanos Valetsiotis
◇ Offenbach: *Hoffmanns Erzählungen*, "Barcarole," duet with A. Bourdacou — Weber: *Oberon*, aria — Verdi: *Aida*, "Ritorna vincitor" and "O terra addio" — Psarouda: Greek song

23 May **Concert** Athens, Parnassos Hall
The students of Maria Trivella's class at the National Conservatory
◇ Weber: *Oberon*, aria — Massenet: *Thaïs*, "Air du miroir"

25 June **Concert** Athens, Olympia Theater
The students of Maria Trivella's class at the National Conservatory
Pianist: Elli Nikolaidou
◇ Arias from Verdi's: *Un Ballo in Maschera*, Act III, M. Callas (Amelia) — Mascagni: *Cavalleria Rusticana*, Act II, M. Callas (Santuzza)

1940

23 February **Concert** Athens, Odeon Concert Hall
The students of Elvira de Hidalgo's class at the National Conservatory
Pianist: Gerassimos Koundouris
◇ Bellini: *Norma*, "Mira o Norma," M. Callas (Norma) in a duet with A. Mandikian

3 April **Concert broadcast** Athens
Maria Callas in duets with Irma Kolassi and Arda Mandikian
◇ Excerpts from Bellini: *Norma* — Verdi: *Aida* — Ponchielli: *La Gioconda*

May **Concert** Athens, Olympia Theater
◇ Excerpts from Verdi: *Un Ballo in Maschera*, Act II — Verdi: *Aida*, Act III

16 June **Concert** Athens, Odeon Concert Hall
The students of Elvira de Hidalgo's class at the National Conservatory
Pianist: Elvira de Hidalgo
◇ Excerpts from Puccini: *Suor Angelica* with M. Callas (Suor Angelica), A. Mandikian, and others

21, 22, 23, 27 October **Concert** Athens, Royal Theater
◇ Excerpts from Shakespeare's *Merchant of Venice* (composer not specified)
M. Callas (?), E. Papadakis (Portia), A. Minotis (Shylock)

27 November ***Boccaccio*** by Franz von Suppé Athens, Royal Theater
M. Callas and N. Galanou (Beatrice), M. Koronis and N. Glinos (Boccaccio)

1941

21 January—9 March ; 3—15 July ***Boccaccio*** by Franz von Suppé Athens, Royal Theater
Conductor: Leonidas Zoras
M. Callas and N. Galanou (Beatrice), M. Koronis and N. Glinos (Boccaccio)

1942

4 July—27 September ***Tosca*** by Giacomo Puccini Athens, Summer Theater at Klafthmonos Square and Opera
Conductor: Lakis Vasilakis and Sotos Vasiliades
M. Callas (Tosca), A. Delendas and L. Kuroussopoulos (Cavaradossi), S. Kalogeras and T. Xirellis (Scarpia)

1943

19, 21, 23, 26 February ; 2, 5, 6, 11, 13, 16, 20 March ***O Protomastoras*** by Manolis Kalomiris Athens, Royal Theater and Herodes Atticus Theater
Pianist: Kostis Mikailidis
A. Remoundou (Protomastoras), N. Galanou, A. Delendas, A. Bourdakou, M. Callas (in the Intermezzo)

The students of Elvira de Hidalgo's class at the National Conservatory

28 February　**Concert**　Smyrna, Sporting Cinema
◇ unknown

22 April　**Concert**　Athens, Casa d'Italia
Maria Callas and Arda Mandikian
Conductor: Georgos Lycoudis
◇ Pergolesi: *Stabat Mater*

17, 31 July　*Tosca* by Giacomo Puccini　Athens, Summer
Theater, Klafthmonos Square
Conductor: Sotos Vassiliadis
M. Callas (Tosca), A. Delendas (Cavaradossi), T. Xirellis
(Scarpia)

21 July　**Solo concert**　Athens, Summer Theater, Costa
Moussouri
Pianist: Andreas Paradis
◇ Arias and songs, Handel: *Atlanta*, "Care Selve" — Rossini:
La Cenerentola — Cilea: *Adriana Lecouvreur* — Verdi: *Il Trovatore* —
Lavda: Greek song
28 August ; 2, 3 September **Concert** Salonika, White Tower
Theater
Pianist: Andreas Paradis
◇ Excerpts from Rossini: *Semiramide* "Bel raggio lusinghier" —
Rossini: *Guglielmo Tell*, "Selva opaca" — Lieder of Schubert and
Brahms

26 September　**Concert**　Athens, Olympia Theater
Pianist: Kostas Kidoniatis
◇ Beethoven: *Fidelio*, "Abscheulicher" — Massenet: *Thaïs*,
"Dis-moi que je suis belle" — Verdi: *Aida*, "Ritorna vincitor" —
Mozart: *Mass in C Minor*, "Et incarnatus est" — Lavda: Greek
song — Turina: Spanish song

12 December　**Concert**　Athens, Kotopouli-Rex Theater
Pianist: Lys Androutsopoulos
◇ Beethoven: *Fidelio*, "Abscheulicher" — Rossini: *Semiramide*,
"Bel raggio lusinghier" — Verdi: *Il Trovatore*, aria — Turina:
"Tamare," Spanish song

1944

22, 23, 25, 27, 30 April ; 4, 7, 10 May　*Tiefland* by Eugène
d'Albert　Athens, Olympia Theater
Conductor: Leonidas Zoras
M. Callas (Marta), Z. Vlachopoulou and M. Papadopoulou
(Nuri), A. Delendas (Pedro), E. Mangliveras (Sebastiano),
N. Mavrakis (Nando)

6, 9, 14, 16, 19, 23, 28 May ; 1, 8 June　*Cavalleria
Rusticana* by Pietro Mascagni　Athens, Olympia Theater
Conductor: Totis Karalivanos
M. Callas (Santuzza), A. Delendas (Turiddu),
T. Tsoumbris (Alfio), M. Kourachani (Lola)

21 May　**Concert**　Athens, Olympia Theater
Maria Callas and others
Conductor: Leonidas Zoras
◇ Excerpts from Bellini: *Norma*, "Casta diva," M. Callas
(Norma)

29, 30 July ; 1, 3, 5, 6 August　*O Protomastoras* by Manolis
Kalomiris　Athens, Herodes Atticus Theater
Conductor: Manolis Kalomiris
M. Callas (Smaragda), A. Delendas (Protomastoras),
E. Mangliveras (ruler), N. Galanou (singer)

14, 15, 17 August　*Fidelio* by Ludwig van Beethoven　Athens,
Herodes Atticus Theater
Conductor: Hans Hoerner
M. Callas (Leonore), A. Delendas (Florestan), E. Mangliveras
(Pizarro), Z. Vlachopoulou (Marcellina)

October　**Concert**　Salonika
For the armed forces
◇ Unknown

1945

14 to 24 March　*Tiefland* by Eugène d'Albert　Athens, Olympia
Theater
Conductor: Leonidas Zoras
M. Callas (Marta), Z. Vlachopoulou (Nuri), A. Delendas
(Pedro), E. Mangliveras (Sebastiano), N. Mavrakis (Nando)

20 March　**Concert for British troups**　Athens, Olympia Theater
Conductor: Totis Karalivanos
◇ Anonymous: "Willow, Willow" — Ronald: "Love, I Have
Won You" — Williams: "On Wenlock Edge"

July　**Concert**　Athens, Kotopouli-Rex Theater
◇ Aria from Italian operas — Lieder by Brahms and Schubert

3 August　**Concert**　Athens, Kotopouli-Rex Theater
Pianist: Alice Lycoudi
◇ Mozart: *Don Giovanni*, Zerlina's aria — Rossini:
Semiramide, "Bel raggio lusinghier" — Verdi: *Aida*, "Ritorna
vincitor" — Verdi: *Il Trovatore*, Leonore's aria — Weber: *Oberon*,
"Ozean, du Ungeheuer" — two Spanish songs — Greek songs
by Kariotakis and Poniridis

5 — 8, 10 — 13 September　*Der Bettelstudent* by Karl Millöcker,
in Italian　Athens, Summer Theater, Alexandras Avenue
Conductor: Antiochos Evanghelatos
M. Callas (Laura), M. Koronis (Simone), M. Molotsos
(Enterich), K. Damasiotis (Palmatica)
M. Callas sang in the first two and probably in two further
performances.

1946 — 1947

From the end of 1946　**Turandot** by Giacomo Puccini　Chicago,
Civic Opera
Rehearsals, production cancelled due to a labor dispute

1947

2, 5, 10, 14, 17 August　*La Gioconda* by Amilcare Ponchielli
Verona, Arena
Conductor: Tullio Serafin
M. Callas (La Gioconda), E. Nicolai (Laura), R. Tucker (Enzo),
C. Tagliabue (Barnaba), N. Rossi-Lemeni (Alvise)

30 Dezember ; 3, 8, 11 January　*Tristan und Isolde* by Richard
Wagner, in Italian　Venice, Teatro La Fenice
Conductor: Tullio Serafin
M. Callas (Isolde), F. Barbieri (Brangäne), F. Tasso (Tristan),
B. Christoff (King Marke), R. Torres (Kurwenal)

1948

29, 31 January ; 3, 8, 10 February　*Turandot* by Giacomo
Puccini　Venice, Teatro La Fenice
Conductor: Nino Sanzogno
M. Callas (Turandot), J. Soler (Calaf), E. Rizzeri (Liù),
B. Caramassi (Timur)

11, 14 March　*Turandot* by Giacomo Puccini　Udine, Teatro
Puccini
Conductor: Oliviero de Fabritiis
M. Callas (Turandot), J. Soler (Calaf), D. Ottani (Liù),
S. Maionica (Timur)

17, 20, 21, 25 April　*La Forza del Destino* by Giuseppe Verdi
Trieste, Politeama Rossetti
Conductor: Mario Parenti
M. Callas (Leonora), G. Vertecchi (Don Alvaro), B. Franci
(Don Carlo), C. Siepi (Oroveso)

12, 14, 16 May   *Tristan und Isolde* by Richard Wagner,
in Italian   Genoa, Teatro Grattacielo
Conductor: Tullio Serafin
M. Callas (Isolde), E. Nicolai (Brangäne), M. Lorenz (Tristan),
N. Rossi-Lemeni (King Mark), R. Torres (Kurwenal)

4, 6, 11 July   *Turandot* by Giacomo Puccini   Rome,
Thermae Caracallae
Conductor: Oliviero de Fabritiis
M. Callas (Turandot), G. Masini (Calaf), V. Montanari (Liù),
G. Flamini (Timur)

27 July ; 1, 5, 9 August   *Turandot* by Giacomo Puccini
Verona, Arena
Conductor: Antonino Votto
M. Callas (Turandot), A. Salvarezza (Calaf), E. Rizzieri (Liù),
N. Rossi-Lemeni (Timur)

11, 14 August   *Turandot* by Giacomo Puccini   Genoa, Teatro
San Felice
Conductor: Angelo Questa
M. Callas (Turandot), M. del Monaco and A. Salvarezza
(Calaf), V. Montanari (Liù), S. Maionica (Timur)

18, 19, 23, 25 September   *Aida* by Giuseppe Verdi   Turin,
Teatro Lirico
Conductor: Tullio Serafin
M. Callas (Aida), R. Turrini (Radames), I. Colasanti and
E. Nicolai (Amneris), E. de Falchi (Amonasro)

19, 21, 24 October   *Aida* by Giuseppe Verdi   Rovigo, Teatro
Sociale
Conductor: Umberto Berretoni
M. Callas (Aida), R. Turrini (Radames), M. Pirazzini (Amneris),
E. Viaro (Amonasro)

30 November ; 5 December   *Norma* by Vincenzo Bellini
Florence, Teatro Comunale
Conductor: Tullio Serafin
M. Callas (Norma), M. Picchi (Pollione), F. Barbieri (Adalgisa),
C. Siepi (Oroveso)

1949

8, 12, 14, 16 January   *Die Walküre* by Richard Wagner,
in Italian   Venice, Teatro La Fenice
Conductor: Tullio Serafin
M. Callas (Brünhilde), J. Magnoni (Sieglinde), A. Pini (Fricka),
G. Voyer (Siegmund), R. Torres (Wotan), E. Dominici
(Hunding)

19, 22, 23 January   *I Puritani* by Vincenzo Bellini   Venice,
Teatro La Fenice
Conductor: Tullio Serafin
M. Callas (Elvira), A. Pirino (Arturo), U. Savarese (Riccardo),
B. Christoff (Giorgio)

28 Januar ; 10 February   *Die Walküre* by Richard Wagner,
in Italian   Palermo, Teatro Massimo
Conductor: Francesco Molinari Pradelli
M. Callas (Brünhilde), J. Magnoni (Sieglinde), L. Cabrera
(Fricka), G. Voyer (Siegmund), G. Neri (Wotan), B. Carmassi
(Hunding)

12, 16, 18, 20 February   *Turandot* by Giacomo Puccini
Naples, Teatro San Carlo
Conductor: Jonel Perlea
M. Callas (Turandot), V. Montanari (Liù), R. Gigli (Calaf),
M. Petri (Timur)

26 February ; 2, 5, 8 March   *Parsifal* by Richard Wagner,
in Italian   Rome, Opera

Conductor: Tullio Serafin
M. Callas (Kundry), H. Beirer (Parsifal), M. Cortis (Amfortas),
C. Siepi (Gurnemanz)

7 March   **Concert broadcast**   Turin, RAI Auditorium
RAI Orchestra, Turin
Conductor: Francesco Molinari Pradelli
◇ Wagner: *Tristan und Isolde*, "Liebestod" — Bellini: *Norma*,
"Casta diva" and "Ah ! bello a me ritorna — Bellini: *I Puritani*,
"Qui la voce" and "Vien diletto" — Verdi: *Aida*, "O cieli azzurri"

20, 29 May ; 11, 22 June   *Turandot* by Giacomo Puccini
Buenos Aires, Teatro Colón
Conductor: Tullio Serafin
M. Callas (Turandot), M. Del Monaco (Calaf), H. Arizmendi
(Liù), J. Zanin and N. Rossi-Lemeni (Timur)

17, 19, 25, 29 June   *Norma* by Vincenzo Bellini   Buenos Aires,
Teatro Colón
Conductor: Tullio Serafin
M. Callas (Norma), A. Vela (Pollione), F. Barbieri (Adalgisa),
N. Rossi-Lemeni (Oroveso)

2 July   *Aida* by Giuseppe Verdi   Buenos Aires, Teatro Colón
Conductor: Tullio Serafin
M. Callas (Aida), A. Vela (Radames), F. Barbieri (Amneris),
V. Damiani (Amonasro)

9 July   **Concert**   Buenos Aires, Teatro Colón
Conductor: Tullio Serafin
◇ Bellini: *Norma*, "Casta diva" — Puccini: *Turandot*,
Act III

18 September   *San Giovanni Battista*, Oratorio by Alessandro
Stradella   Perugia, Chiesa di San Pietro
Conductor: Gabriele Santini
M. Callas (Figlia di Erode), R. Corsi (Madre di Erode),
M. Pirazzini (San Giovanni Battista), C. Siepi (Erode)

31 October   **Concert**   Verona, Teatro Nuovo
Conductor: Umberto Berrettoni
◇ Arias from Bellini: *Norma* — Wagner: *Tristan und Isolde* —
Bellini: *I Puritani* — Meyerbeer: *Dinorah* — Verdi: *La Traviata*

24 November   **Concert**   Turin, RAI Auditorium
RAI Orchestra, Turin
Conductor: Baroni
◇ Puccini: *Tosca*, Act II — Massenet: *Manon Lescaut*, Act IV

20, 22, 27 December   *Nabucco* by Giuseppe Verdi   Naples,
Teatro San Carlo
Conductor: Vittorio Gui
Maria Callas (Abigaille), A. Pini (Fenena), G. Sinimberghi
(Ismaele), G. Bechi (Nabucco), L. Neroni (Zaccaria)

1950

13, 15, 19 January   *Norma* by Vincenzo Bellini   Venice, Teatro
La Fenice
Conductor: Antonino Votto
M. Callas (Norma), G. Penno (Pollione), E. Nicolai (Adalgisa),
T. Pasero (Oroveso)

2, 7 February   *Aida* by Giuseppe Verdi   Brescia, Teatro Grande
Conductor: Alberto Erede
M. Callas (Aida), M. del Monaco (Radames), A. Pini (Amneris),
A. Protti (Amonasro)

6, 9, 19, 25, 28 February   *Tristan und Isolde* by Richard
Wagner, in Italian   Rome, Opera
Conductor: Tullio Serafin
M. Callas (Isolde), E. Nicolai (Brangäne), A. Seider (Tristan),
B. Franchi (Kurwenal), G. Neri (King Mark)

23, 26 February ; 2, 4, 7 March   *Norma* by Vincenzo Bellini
Rome, Opera
Conductor: Tullio Serafin
M. Callas (Norma), G. Masini (Pollione), E. Stignani
(Adalgisa), G. Neri (Oroveso)

13 March   **Concert broadcast**   Turin, RAI Auditorium
Maria Callas and Cesare Siepi
RAI Orchestra, Turin
Conductor: Alfredo Simonetto
◇ Weber: *Oberon*, "Ozean, du Ungeheuer" — Verdi: *La
Traviata*, "Ah fors'è lui" and "Sempre libera" — Verdi: *Il Trovatore*,
"D'amor sull'ali rosee" — Meyerbeer: *Dinorah*, "Ombra leggera"

16, 19, 22, 25 March   *Norma* by Vincenzo Bellini   Catania,
Teatro Massimo Bellini
Conductor: Umberto Berrettoni
M. Callas (Norma), M. Picchi (Pollione), J. Gardino (Adalgisa),
M. Stefanoni (Oroveso)

12, 15, 18 April   *Aida* by Giuseppe Verdi   Milan, La Scala
Conductor: Franco Capuana
M. Callas (Aida), M. del Monaco (Radames), F. Barbieri
(Amneris), R. de Falchi and A. Protti (Amonasro)

27, 30 April ; 2, 4 May   *Aida* by Giuseppe Verdi   Naples,
Teatro San Carlo
Conductor: Tullio Serafin
M. Callas (Aida), M. Picchi (Radames), E. Stignani (Amneris),
U. Savarese (Amonasro)

23, 27 May   *Norma* by Vincenzo Bellini   Mexico City, Palacio
de las Bellas Artes
Conductor: Guido Picco
M. Callas (Norma), K. Baum (Pollione), G. Simionato
(Adalgisa), N. Moscona (Oroveso)

30 May ; 8, 10 June   *Aida* by Giuseppe Verdi   Mexico City,
Palacio de las Bellas Artes
Conductor: Guido Picco
M. Callas (Aida), K. Baum and M. Filippeschi (Radames),
G. Simionato (Amneris), R. Weede (Amonasro)

8, 10 June   *Tosca* by Giacomo Puccini   Mexico City, Palacio de
las Bellas Artes
Conductor: Umberto Mugnai
M. Callas (Tosca), M. Filippeschi (Mario), R. Weede (Scarpia)

20, 24, 27 June   *Il Trovatore* by Giuseppe Verdi   Mexico City,
Palacio de las Bellas Artes
Conductor: Guido Picco
M. Callas (Leonora), K. Baum (Manrico), I. Petroff and
L. Warren (Conte di Luna), N. Moscona (Ferrando)

22 September   *Tosca* by Giacomo Puccini   Salsomaggiore,
Teatro Nuovo
Conductor: Angelo Questa
M. Callas (Tosca), R. Pelizzoni (Mario), G. Inghilleri (Scarpia)

24 September   *Tosca* by Giacomo Puccini   Bologna,
Teatro Duse
Conductor: Angelo Questa
M. Callas (Tosca), R. Turrini (Mario), R. Azzolini (Scarpia)

2 October   *Aida* by Giuseppe Verdi   Rome, Opera
Conductor: Vincenzo Bellezza
M. Callas (Aida), M. Picchi (Radames), E. Stignani (Amneris),
R. de Falchi (Amonasro)

7, 8 October   *Tosca* by Giacomo Puccini   Pisa, Teatro
Comunale Giuseppe Verdi
Conductor: Riccardo Santarelli
M. Callas (Tosca), G. Masini (Mario), A. Poli (Scarpia)

19, 22, 25, 29 October   *Il Turco in Italia* by Giacomo Rossini
Rome, Teatro Eliseo
Conductor: Gianandrea Gavazzeni
M. Callas (Fiorilla), S. Bruscantini (Selim), A. Canali (Zaida),
C. Valletti (Narciso), M. Stabile (Prosdocimo)

20, 21 November   *Parsifal* (concert performance) by Richard
Wagner, in Italian   Rome, RAI Studio
RAI Orchestra, Rome
Conductor: Vittorio Gui
M. Callas (Kundry), A. Baldelli (Parsifal), B. Christoff
(Gurnemanz), R. Panerai (Amfortas), G. Modesti (Klingsor)
20 November: Act I ; 21 November: Act II

1951

14, 16, 20 January   *La Traviata* by Giuseppe Verdi   Florence,
Teatro Comunale
Conductor: Tullio Serafin
M. Callas (Violetta), F. Albanese (Alfredo), E. Mascherini
(Germont)

27, 30 January ; 1 February   *Il Trovatore* by Giuseppe Verdi
Naples, Teatro San Carlo
Conductor: Tullio Serafin
M. Callas (Leonora), G. Lauri Volpi and G. Vertecchi
(Manrico), C. Elmo (Azucena), P. Silveri (Conte di Luna),
I. Tajo (Ferrando)

15, 20 February   *Norma* by Vincenzo Bellini   Palermo, Teatro
Massimo
Conductor: Franco Ghione
M. Callas (Norma), R. Gavarini (Pollione), E. Nicolai
(Adalgisa), G. Neri (Oroveso)

28 February   *Aida* by Giuseppe Verdi   Reggio Calabria, Teatro
Comunale
Conductor: Federico del Cupolo
M. Callas (Aida), J. Soler (Radames), M. Pirazzini (Amneris),
A. Manca-Serra (Amonasro)

12 March   **Concert broadcast**   Turin, RAI Auditorium
Maria Callas and Sesto Bruscantini
RAI Orchestra, Turin
Conductor: Ermanno Wolf-Ferrari
◇ Weber: *Der Freischütz*, Agathe's aria — Thomas: *Mignon*, "Io
sono Titania" — Verdi: *Un Ballo in Maschera*, "Ecco l'orrido
campi" and "Ma dall'arido stelo" — Proch: Variazioni

14, 18 March   *La Traviata* by Giuseppe Verdi   Cagliari,
Teatro Massimo
Conductor: Francesco Molinari Pradelli
M. Callas (Violetta), G. Campora (Alfredo), A. Poli (Germont)

21 April   **Concert**   Trieste, Teatro Giuseppe Verdi
Maria Callas with Tito Schipa, Dolores Wilson, and
M. Tommasini
Orchestra Filharmonica Triestina
Conductor: Armando La Rosa Parodi
◇ Bellini: *Norma*, "Casta diva" — Bellini: *I Puritani*, "Qui la
voce" — Verdi: *Aida*, "O cieli azzurri" — Verdi: *La Traviata*,
"Ah ! fors' è lui" and "Sempre libera"

26, 30 May ; 2, 5 June   *Les Vêpres Siciliennes* by Giuseppe
Verdi   Florence, Teatro Comunale
Conductor: Erich Kleiber
M. Callas (Elena), E. Mascherini (Monforte), G. Bardi-Kokolios
(Arrigo), B. Christoff (Procida)

9, 10 June   *Orfeo ed Euridice* by Joseph Haydn   Florence,
Teatro alla Pergola
Conductor: Erich Kleiber
M. Callas (Euridice), T. Tygesen (Orfeo), B. Christoff (Creonte)

11 June   **Concert**   Florence, Grand Hotel
Pianist: Bruno Bartoletti
◇ Bellini: *Norma*, "Casta diva" — Meyerbeer: *Dinorah*, "Ombra leggera" — Verdi: *Aida*, "O cieli azzurri" — Proch: Variazioni — Thomas: *Mignon*, polka — Verdi: *La Traviata*, "Ah ! fors' è lui" and "Sempre libera"

3, 7, 10 July   *Aida* by Guiseppe Verdi   Mexico City, Palacio de las Bellas Artes
Conductor: Oliviero de Fabritiis
M. Callas (Aida), M. del Monaco (Radames), O. Dominguez (Amneris), G. Taddei (Amonasro)

15 July   **Concert broadcast**   Mexico City, Radio XEW
Conductor: Oliviero de Fabritiis
◇ Verdi: *La Forza del Destino*, "Pace, pace mio Dio" — Verdi: *Un Ballo in Maschera*, "Morrò, ma prima in grazia"

17, 19, 21, 22 July   *La Traviata* by Guiseppe Verdi   Mexico City, Palacio de las Bellas Artes
Conductor: Oliviero de Fabritiis
M. Callas (Violetta), C. Valletti (Alfredo), G. Taddei and C. Morelli (Germont)

7 September   *Norma* by Vincenzo Bellini   Sao Paolo, Teatro Municipal
Conductor: Tullio Serafin
M. Callas (Norma), M. Picchi (Pollione), F. Barbieri (Adalgisa), N. Rossi-Lemeni (Oroveso)

9 September   *La Traviata* by Giuseppe Verdi   Sao Paolo, Teatro Municipal
Conductor: Tullio Serafin
M. Callas (Violetta), G. di Stefano (Alfredo), T. Gobbi (Germont)

12, 16 September   *Norma* by Vincenzo Bellini   Rio de Janeiro, Teatro Municipal
Conductor: Antonino Votto
M. Callas (Norma), M. Picchi (Pollione), E. Nicolai (Adalgisa), B. Christoff (Oroveso)

14 September   **Concert**   Rio de Janeiro, Teatro Municipal
Maria Callas, Renata Tebaldi, Paolo Silveri, and Boris Christoff
◇ Verdi: *La Traviata*, "Ah ! fors'è lui" — Verdi: *Aida*, "O cieli azzurri"

24 September   *Tosca* by Giacomo Puccini   Rio de Janeiro, Teatro Municipal
Conductor: Antonino Votto
M. Callas (Tosca), G. Poggi (Mario), P. Silveri (Scarpia)

28, 30 September   *La Traviata* by Giuseppe Verdi   Rio de Janeiro, Teatro Municipal
Conductor: Nino Gaioni
M. Callas (Violetta), G. Poggi (Alfredo), A. Salsedo (Germont)

20, 23 October   *La Traviata* by Giuseppe Verdi   Bergamo, Teatro Gaetano Donizetti
Conductor: Carlo Maria Giulini
M. Callas (Violetta), G. Prandelli (Alfredo), G. Fabbri (Germont)

3, 6, 17, 20 November   *Norma* by Vincenzo Bellini   Catania, Teatro Massimo Bellini
Conductor: Franco Ghione
M. Callas (Norma), G. Penno (Pollione), G. Simionato (Adalgisa), B. Christoff and L. Wolovski (Oroveso)

8, 11, 13, 16 November   *I Puritani* by Vincenzo Bellini   Catania, Teatro Massimo Bellini
Conductor: Ermanno Wolf-Ferrari
M. Callas (Elvira), W. Wenkow (Arturo), C. Tagliabue (Riccardo), B. Christoff (Giorgio)

7, 9, 12, 16, 19, 27 December   *Les Vêpres Siciliennes* by Giuseppe Verdi   Milan, La Scala
Conductor: Victor de Sabata and Argeo Quadri
M. Callas (Elena), E. Conley (Arrigo), E. Mascherini (Monfort), B. Christoff and G. Modesti (Procida)

29 December   *La Traviata* by Giuseppe Verdi   Parma, Teatro Reggio
Conductor: Oliviero de Fabritiis
M. Callas (Violetta), A. Pola (Alfredo), U. Savarese (Germont)

1952

3 January   *Les Vêpres Siciliennes* by Giuseppe Verdi   Milan, La Scala
Conductor: Victor de Sabata and Argeo Quadri
M. Callas (Elena), E. Conley (Arrigo), E. Mascherini (Monfort), B. Christoff and G. Modesti (Procida)

9, 11 January   *I Puritani* by Vincenzo Bellini   Florence, Teatro Comunale
Conductor: Tullio Serafin
M. Callas (Elvira), E. Conley (Arturo), C. Tagliabue (Riccardo), N. Rossi-Lemeni (Giorgio)

16, 19, 23, 27, 29 January ; 2, 7, 10 February ; 14 April   *Norma* by Vincenzo Bellini   Milan, La Scala
Conductor: Franco Ghione
M. Callas (Norma), G. Penno (Pollione), E. Stignani (Adalgisa), N. Rossi-Lemeni (Oroveso)

8 February   **Concert**   Milan, Circolo della Stampa
Pianist: P. Tonini
◇ Excerpts from Verdi: *La Traviata* — Bellini: *I Puritani*, Mad Scene

18 February   **Concert broadcast**   Rome, RAI Studio
Maria Callas and Nicola Filacuridi
RAI Orchestra
Conductor: Oliviero de Fabritiis
◇ Verdi: *Macbeth*, "Vieni, t'affretta" and "Or tutti sorgete" — Donizetti: *Lucia di Lammermoor*, "Il dolce suono" and first part of the Mad Scene — Verdi *Nabucco*, "Ben io t'invenni," "Anch'io dischiuso un giorno" and "Salgo già" — Delibes: *Lakmé*, "Dov'è l'indiana bruna"

8, 12, 14, 16 March   *La Traviata* by Giuseppe Verdi   Catania, Teatro Massimo Bellini
Conductor: Francesco Molinari Pradelli
M. Callas (Violetta), G. Campora (Alfredo), E. Mascherini (Germont)

2, 5, 7, 9 April   *Die Entführung aus dem Serail* by Wolfgang Amadeus Mozart   Milan, La Scala
Conductor: Jonel Perlea
M. Callas (Constanza), S. Baccaloni (Osmin), T. Menotti and F. Duval (Blondchen), G. Prandelli (Belmonte), P. Munteano (Pedrillo)

26, 29 April ; 4 May   *Armida* by Gioacchino Rossini   Florence, Teatro Comunale
Conductor: Tullio Serafin
M. Callas (Armida), F. Albanese (Rinaldo), A. Ziliani (Goffredo), A. Salvarezza (Eustazio), G. Raimondi (Carlo), M. Filippeschi (Fernando)

2, 6, 11 May   *I Puritani* by Vincenzo Bellini   Rome, Opera
Conductor: Gabriele Santini
M. Callas (Elvira), G. Lauri Volpi and A. Pirini (Arturo), P. Silveri (Riccardo), G. Neri (Giorgio)

29, 31 May   *I Puritani* by Vincenzo Bellini   Mexico City,
Palacio de las Bellas Artes
Conductor: Guido Picco
M. Callas (Elvira), G. di Stefano (Arturo), P. Campolonghi
(Riccardo), R. Silva (Giorgio)

3, 7 June   *La Traviata* by Giuseppe Verdi   Mexico City, Palacio
de las Bellas Artes
Conductor: Umberto Mugnai
M. Callas (Violetta), G. di Stefano (Alfredo), P. Campolonghi
(Germont)

10, 14, 26 June   *Lucia di Lammermoor* by Gaetano Donizetti
Mexico City, Palacio de las Bellas Artes
Conductor: Guido Picco
M. Callas (Lucia), G. di Stefano (Edgardo), P. Campolonghi
(Enrico)

17, 21 June   *Rigoletto* by Giuseppe Verdi   Mexico City, Palacio
de las Bellas Artes
Conductor: Umberto Mugnai
M. Callas (Gilda), G. di Stefano (Duca), P. Campolonghi
(Rigoletto)

28 June ; 1 July   *Tosca* by Giacomo Puccini   Mexico City,
Palacio de las Bellas Artes
Conductor: Guido Picco
M. Callas (Tosca), G. di Stefano (Mario), P. Campolonghi
(Scarpia)

19, 23 July   *La Gioconda* by Amilcare Ponchielli   Verona Arena
Conductor: Antonino Votto
M. Callas (Gioconda), C. Poggi (Enzo), E. Nicolai (Laura),
G. Inghilleri (Barnaba), I. Tajo (Alvise)

2, 5, 10, 14 August   *La Traviata* by Giuseppe Verdi
Verona, Arena
Conductor: Francesco Molinari Pradelli
M. Callas (Violetta), G. Campora (Alfredo), E. Mascherini
(Germont)

8, 10, 13, 18, 20 November   *Norma* by Vincenzo Bellini
London, Covent Garden
Conductor: Vittorio Gui and John Pritchard
M. Callas (Norma), M. Picchi (Pollione), E. Stignani
(Adalgisa), G. Vaghi (Oroveso)

7, 9, 11, 14, 17 December   *Macbeth* by Giuseppe Verdi   Milan,
La Scala
Conductor: Victor de Sabata
M. Callas (Lady Macbeth), E. Mascherini (Macbeth), C. Penno
(Macduff), I. Tajo und G. Modesti (Banco)

26, 28, 30 December   *La Gioconda* by Amilcare Ponchielli
Milan, La Scala
Conductor: Antonino Votto
M. Callas (Gioconda), G. di Stefano (Enzo), E. Stignani
(Laura), C. Tagliabue (Barnaba), I. Tajo und G. Modesti
(Alvise)

1953

1, 3 January, 19 February   *La Gioconda* by Amilcare Ponchielli
Milan, La Scala
Conductor: Antonino Votto
M. Callas (Gioconda), G. di Stefano (Enzo), E. Stignani
(Laura), C. Tagliabue (Barnaba), I. Tajo (Alvise)

8, 10 January   *La Traviata* by Giuseppe Verdi   Venice,
Teatro La Fenice
Conductor: Angelo Questa
M. Callas (Violetta), F. Albanese (Alfredo), U. Savarese and
C. Tagliabue (Germont)

15, 18, 21 January   *La Traviata* by Giuseppe Verdi   Rome,
Opera
Conductor: Gabriele Santini
M. Callas (Violetta), F. Albanese (Alfredo), U. Savarese
(Germont)

25, 28 January ; 5, 8 February   *Lucia di Lammermoor* by Gaetano
Donizetti   Florence, Theatro Comunale
Conductor: Franco Ghione
M. Callas (Lucia), G. Lauri Volpi und G. di Stefano (Edgardo),
E. Bastianini (Enrico)

23, 26, 28 February ; 24, 29 March   *Il Trovatore* by Giuseppe
Verdi   Milan, La Scala
Conductor: Antonino Votto
M. Callas (Leonora), G. Penno (Manrico), E. Stignani
(Asucena), C. Tagliabue (Conte di Luna), G. Modesti
(Ferrando)

14, 17 March   *Lucia di Lammermoor* by Gaetano Donizetti
Genoa, Teatro Carlo Felice
Conductor: Franco Ghione
M. Callas (Lucia), G. di Stefano (Edgardo), E. Mascherini (Enrico)

9, 12, 15, 18 April   *Norma* by Vincenzo Bellini   Rome, Opera
Conductor: Gabriele Santini
M. Callas (Norma), F. Corelli (Pollione), F. Barbieri (Adalgisa),
G. Neri (Oroveso)

21, 23 April   *Lucia di Lammermoor* by Gaetano Donizetti
Catania, Teatro Massimo Bellini
Conductor: Oliviero de Fabritiis
M. Callas (Lucia), R. Turrini (Edgardo), G. Taddei (Enrico)

7, 10, 12 May   *Medea* by Luigi Cherubini   Florence,
Teatro Comunale
Conductor: Vittorio Gui
M. Callas (Medea), C. Guichandut (Giasone), G. Tucci
(Glauce), F. Barbieri (Neris), M. Petri (Creonte)

16 May   **Concert**   Rome, Palazzo Pio
Conductor: Oliviero de Fabritiis
◇ Verdi: *Il Trovatore*, "D'amor sull'ali rosee" — Verdi: *La Forza
del Destino*, "Pace, pace, mio Dio" — Meyerbeer: *Dinorah*,
"Ombra leggera"

19, 21, 24 May   *Lucia di Lammermoor* by Gaetano Donizetti
Rome, Opera
Conductor: Gianandrea Gavazzeni
M. Callas (Lucia), G. Poggi (Edgardo), G. Guelfi (Enrico)

4, 6, 10 June   *Aida* by Giuseppe Verdi   London, Covent Garden
Conductor: John Barbirolli
M. Callas (Aida), K. Baum (Radames), G. Simionato (Amneris),
J. Walters (Amonasro)

15, 17, 20, 23 June   *Norma* by Vincenzo Bellini   London,
Covent Garden
Conductor: John Pritchard
M. Callas (Norma), M. Picchi (Pollione), G. Simionato
(Adalgisa), G. Neri (Oroveso)

26, 29 June ; 1 July   *Il Trovatore* by Giuseppe Verdi   London,
Covent Garden
Conductor: Alberto Erede
M. Callas (Leonora), J. Johnston (Manrico), G. Simionato
(Asucena), J. Walters (Conte di Luna), M. Langdon (Ferrando)

23, 25, 28, 30 July ; 8 August   *Aida* by Giuseppe Verdi   Verona,
Arena
Conductor: Tullio Serafin and Franco Ghione
M. Callas (Aida), M. del Monaco, M. Filippeschi and
P. Zambruno (Radames), E. Nicolai and M. Pirazzini (Amneris),
A. Protti and M. Malaspina (Amonasro)

15 August   *Il Trovatore* by Giuseppe Verdi   Verona, Arena
Conductor: Francesco Molinari Pradelli
M. Callas (Leonora), P. Zambruno (Manrico), L. Danieli
(Asucena), A. Protti (Conte di Luna), S. Maionica (Ferrando)

19, 20, 23, 29 November   *Norma* by Vincenzo Bellini   Trieste,
Teatro Giuseppe Verdi
Conductor: Antonino Votto
M. Callas (Norma), F. Corelli (Pollione), E. Nicolai (Adalgisa),
B. Christoff (Oroveso)

10, 12, 29 December   *Medea* by Luigi Cherubini   Milan,
La Scala
Conductor: Leonard Bernstein
Director: Margherita Wallmann
M. Callas (Medea), G. Penno (Giasone), M. L. Nache
(Glauce), F. Barbieri (Neris), G. Modesti (Creonte)

16, 19, 23 December   *Il Trovatore* by Giuseppe Verdi   Rome,
Opera
Conductor: Gabriele Santini
M. Callas (Leonora), G. Lauri Volpi (Manrico), F. Barbieri and
M. Pirazzini (Asucena), P. Silveri (Conte di Luna), G. Neri
(Ferrando)

1954

2, 6 January   *Medea* by Luigi Cherubini   Milan, La Scala
Conductor: Leonard Bernstein
Director: Margherita Wallmann
M. Callas (Medea), G. Penno (Giasone), M. L. Nache
(Glauce), E. Barbieri (Neris), G. Modesti (Creonte)

18, 21, 24, 27, 31 January ; 5, 7 February   *Lucia di Lammermoor*
by Gaetano Donizetti   Milan, La Scala
Conductor and director: Herbert von Karajan
M. Callas (Lucia), G. di Stefano and G. Poggi (Edgardo),
R. Panerai (Enrico)

13, 16, 21 February   *Lucia di Lammermoor* by Gaetano
Donizetti   Venice, Teatro La Fenice
Conductor: Angelo Questa
M. Callas (Lucia), L. Infantino (Edgardo), E. Bastianini (Enrico)

2, 4, 7 March   *Medea* by Luigi Cherubini   Venice,
Teatro La Fenice
Conductor: Vittorio Gui
M. Callas (Medea), R. Gavarini (Giasone), G. Tucci (Glauce),
M. Pirazzini (Neris), G. Tozzi (Creonte)

10, 15, 17 March   *Tosca* by Giacomo Puccini   Genoa,
Teatro Carlo Felice
Conductor: Franco Ghione
M. Callas (Tosca), M. Ortica (Mario), G. Guelfi (Scarpia)

4, 6, 15, 20 April   *Alceste* by Christoph Willibald Gluck
Milan, La Scala
Conductor: Carlo Maria Giulini
Director: Margherita Wallmann
M. Callas (Alceste), R. Gavarini (Admeto), P. Silveri (Priest),
R. Panerai (Apollo)

12, 17, 23, 25, 27 April   *Don Carlo* by Giuseppe Verdi   Milan,
La Scala
Conductor: Antonino Votto
M. Callas (Elisabeth), M. Ortica (Don Carlos), N. Rossi-
Lemeni (Philipp), E. Stignani (Eboli), E. Mascherini
(Grand Inquisitor)

23, 26 May   *La Forza del Destino* by Giuseppe Verdi   Ravenna,
Teatro Alighieri
Conductor: Franco Ghione
M. Callas (Leonora), M. del Monaco (Don Alvaro), A. Protti

(Don Carlo), G. Modesti (Padre Guardiano), J. Cardino
(Preziosilla)

15, 20, 25 July   *Mefistofele* by Arrigo Boito   Verona, Arena
Conductor: Antonino Votto
M. Callas (Margherita), G. di Stefano and F. Tagliavini (Faust),
D. de Cecco and A. de Cavalieri (Elena), N. Rossi-Lemeni
(Mefistofele)

6, 9 October   *Lucia di Lammermoor* by Gaetano Donizetti
Bergamo, Teatro Donizetti
Conductor: Francesco Molinari Pradelli
M. Callas (Lucia), F. Tagliavini (Edgardo), U. Savarese (Enrico)

1, 5 November   *Norma* by Vincenzo Bellini   Chicago, Lyric
Theater
Conductor: Nicola Rescigno
M. Callas (Norma), M. Picchi (Pollione), G. Simionato
(Adalgisa), N. Rossi-Lemeni (Oroveso)

8, 12 November   *La Traviata* by Giuseppe Verdi   Chicago,
Lyric Theater
Conductor: Nicola Rescigno
M. Callas (Violetta), L. Simoneau (Alfredo), T. Gobbi
(Germont)

15, 17 November   *Lucia di Lammermoor* by Gaetano
Donizetti   Chicago, Lyric Theater
Conductor: Nicola Rescigno
M. Callas (Lucia), G. di Stefano (Edgardo), G. Guelfi (Enrico)

7, 9, 12, 16, 18 December   *La Vestale* by Gaspare Spontini
Milan, La Scala
Conductor: Antonino Votto
Director: Luchino Visconti
M. Callas (Giulia), E. Stignani (La Grande Vestale), F. Corelli
(Licinio), E. Sordello (Cinna), N. Rossi-Lemeni (Console)

27 December   **Concert broadcast**   San Remo,
Teatro del Casinò
Maria Callas and Benjamin Gigli
RAI Orchester, Milan
Conductor: Alfredo Simonetto
◇ Mozart: *Die Entführung aus dem Serail*, "Tutte le torture" —
Meyerbeer: *Dinorah*, "Ombra leggera" — Charpentier: *Louise*,
"Depuis le jour" — Rossini: *Armida*, "D'amor al dolce impero"

1955

8, 10, 13, 16 January ; 3, 6 February   *Andrea Chenier* by
Umberto Giordano   Milan, La Scala
Conductor: Antonino Votto
M. Callas (Maddalena), M. del Monaco, and M. Ortica
(Chenier), A. Protti and Giuseppe Taddei (Gérard)

22, 25, 27, 30 January   *Medea* by Luigi Cherubini
Rome, Opera
Conductor: Gabriele Santini
Director: Margherita Wallmann
M. Callas (Medea), F. Albanese (Giasone), G. Tucci (Glauce),
F. Barbieri (Neris), B. Christoff (Creonte)

5, 8, 13, 16, 19, 24, 30 March ; 12, 24, 27 April   *La Sonnambula*
by Vincenzo Bellini   Milan, La Scala
Conductor: Leonard Bernstein
Director: Luchino Visconti
M. Callas (Amina), C. Valletti (Elvino), G. Modesti and
V. Zaccaria (Rodolfo)

15, 18, 21, 23 April ; 4 May   *Il Turco in Italia* by Gioacchino
Rossini   Milan, La Scala
Conductor: Nicola Rescigno
M. Callas (Fiorilla), N. Rossi-Lemeni (Selim), C. Valletti
(Narciso), J. Gardino (Zaida), M. Stabile (Prosdocimo)

28, 31 May ; 5, 7 June   *La Traviata* by Giuseppe Verdi   Milan,
La Scala
Conductor: Carlo Maria Giulini
Director: Luchino Visconti
M. Callas (Violetta), G. di Stefano and G. Prandelli (Alfredo),
G. Bastianini (Germont)

29 June   *Norma* (concert broadcast) by Vincenzo Bellini   Rome,
RAI Studio
RAI Orchestra and Chorus, Rome
Conductor: Tullio Serafin
M. Callas (Norma), M. del Monaco (Pollione), E. Stignani
(Adalgisa), G. Modesti (Oroveso)

29 September ; 2 October   *Lucia di Lammermoor* by Gaetano
Donizetti   Berlin, Staatsoper
Conductor and director: Herbert von Karajan
M. Callas (Lucia), G. di Stefano and G. Zampieri (Edgardo),
R. Panerai (Enrico)

31 October ; 2 November   *I Puritani* by Vincenzo Bellini
Chicago, Lyric Theater
Conductor: Nicola Rescigno
M. Callas (Elvira), G. di Stefano (Arturo), E. Bastianini
(Riccardo), N. Rossi-Lemeni (Giorgio)

5, 8 November   *Il Trovatore* by Giuseppe Verdi   Chicago,
Lyric Theater
Conductor: Nicola Rescigno
M. Callas (Leonora), J. Bjorling (Manrico), E. Stignani and
C. Turner (Asucena), E. Bastiani and Robert Weede (Conte di
Luna), W. Wildermann (Ferrando)

11, 14, 17 November   *Madame Butterfly* by Giacomo Puccini
Chicago, Lyric Theater
Conductor: Nicola Rescigno
M. Callas (Cio-Cio-San), G. di Stefano (Pinkerton), R. Weede
(Sharpless), E. Alberts (Suzuki)

7, 9, 11, 14, 17, 21 December   *Norma* by Vincenzo Bellini
Milan, La Scala
Conductor: Antonino Votto
Director: Margherita Wallmann
M. Callas (Norma), M. del Monaco (Pollione), G. Simionato
and E. Nicolai (Adalgisa), N. Zaccaria (Oroveso)

1956

1, 5, 8 January   *Norma* by Vincenzo Bellini   Milan, La Scala
Conductor: Antonino Votto
Director: Margherita Wallmann
M. Callas (Norma), M. del Monaco (Pollione), G. Simionato
and E. Nicolai (Adalgisa), N. Zaccaria (Oroveso)

19, 23, 26, 29 January ; 2, 15, 18, 26 February ; 9 March ;
4, 5, 18, 21, 25, 27, 29 April ; 6 May   *La Traviata* by
Giuseppe Verdi   Milan, La Scala
Conductor: Carlo Maria Giulini and Antonio Tonini
M. Callas (Violetta), G. Raimondi (Alfredo), A. Protti,
C. Tagliabue and A. Colzani (Germont)

16, 21 February ; 3, 6, 15 March   *Il Barbiere di Siviglia* by
Gioacchino Rossini   Milan, La Scala
Conductor: Carlo Maria Giulini
M. Callas (Rosina), T. Gobbi (Figaro), L. Alva and N. Monti
(Almaviva), N. Rossi-Lemeni (Don Basilio), M. Louise and
C. Badioli (Don Bartolo)

22, 24, 27 March   *Lucia di Lammermoor* by Gaetano
Donizetti   Naples, Teatro San Carlo
Conductor: Francesco Molinari Pradelli
M. Callas (Lucia), G. Raimondi (Edgardo), R. Panerai (Enrico)

21, 23, 27, 30 May   *Fedora* by Umberto Giordano   Milan,
La Scala
Conductor: Gianandrea Gavazzeni
M. Callas (Fedora), F. Corelli (Loris), S. Zanolli (Olga),
A. Colzani (De Sirieux), P. Montarsolo (Cyrill)

12, 14, 16 June   *Lucia di Lammermoor* by Gaetano Donizetti
Vienna, Staatsoper
Conductor: Herbert von Karajan
M. Callas (Lucia), G. di Stefano (Edgardo), R. Panerai (Enrico)

27 September   **Concert broadcast**   Milan, RAI Studio
Maria Callas and Gianni Raimondi
RAI Orchestra, Milan
Conductor: Alfredo Simonetto
◇ Spontini: *La Vestale*, "Tu che invoco" — Rossini:
Semiramide, "Bel raggio lusinghier" — Thomas: *Hamlet*, "A vos
jeux, mes amis" and "Ed ora voi canterò" — Bellini: *I Puritani*,
"Vieni al tempio"

29 October ; 3, 7, 10, 22 November   *Norma* by Vincenzo
Bellini   New York, Metropolitan Opera
Conductor: Fausto Cleva
M. Callas (Norma), M. del Monaco and K. Baum (Pollione),
F. Barbieri (Adalgisa), C. Siepi (Oroveso)

15, 19 November   *Tosca* by Giacomo Puccini   New York,
Metropolitan Opera
Conductor: Dimitri Mitropoulos
M. Callas (Tosca), G. Campora (Mario), G. London
(Scarpia)

25 November   **Television broadcast**   (Ed Sullivan Show)
New York, Studio 28, CBS
Maria Callas and George London
Conductor: Dimitri Mitropoulos
◇ Excerpts from Puccini: *Tosca*, Act II

27 November   *Norma* by Vincenzo Bellini   Philadelphia,
Academy of Music
Conductor: Fausto Cleva
M. Callas (Norma), K. Baum (Pollione), F. Barbieri (Adalgisa),
N. Moscona (Oroveso)

3, 8, 14, 19 December   *Lucia di Lammermoor* by Gaetano
Donizetti   New York, Metropolitan Opera
Conductor: Fausto Cleva
M. Callas (Lucia), G. Campora and R. Tucker (Edgardo),
E. Sordello and F. Valentino (Enrico)

17 December   **Concert**   Washington, Italian Embassy
Pianist: Theodore Schaefer
◇ Verdi: *Il Trovatore*, "D'amor sull'ali rosee — Bellini: *Norma*,
"Casta diva" — Verdi: *La Traviata*, "Ah! fors'è lui" — Puccini:
Tosca, "Vissi d'arte" — Donizetti: *Lucia di Lammermoor*, "Regnava
nel silenzio"

1957

15 January   **Concert**   Chicago, Lyric Theater
Chicago Symphony Orchestra
Conductor: Fausto Cleva
◇ Bellini: *La Sonnambula*, "Ah, non credea mirarti —
Meyerbeer: *Dinorah*, "Ombra leggera" — Puccini: *Turandot*,
"In questa reggia" — Bellini: *Norma*, "Casta diva" — Verdi:
Il Trovatore, "D'amor sull'ali rosee" — Donizetti: *Lucia di
Lammermoor*, "Il dolce suono" and the Mad Scene

2, 6 February   *Norma* by Vincenzo Bellini   London, Covent
Garden
Conductor: John Pritchard
M. Callas (Norma), G. Vertecchi (Pollione), E. Stignani
(Adalgisa), N. Zaccaria (Oroveso)

2, 7, 10, 12, 17, 20 March   *La Sonnambula* by Vincenzo
Bellini   Milan, La Scala
Conductor: Antonino Votto
Director: Luchino Visconti
M. Callas (Amina), M. Spina and N. Monti (Elvino),
N. Zaccaria (Rodolfo)

14, 17, 20, 24, 27, 30 April ; 5 May   *Anna Bolena* by Gaetano
Donizetti   Milan, La Scala
Conductor: Gianandrea Gavazzeni
Director: Luchino Visconti
M. Callas (Anna Bolena), G. Simionato (Seymour),
G. Raimondi (Percy), N. Rossi-Lemeni (Enrico)

1, 3, 5, 10 June   *Iphigénie en Tauride* by Christoph Willibald
Gluck   Milan, La Scala
Conductor: Nino Sanzogno
M. Callas (Iphigénie), F. Albanese (Pilade), D. Dondi (Oreste),
A. Golzani (Toante), F. Cossotto (Artemide)

19 June   **Concert**   Zurich, Tonhalle
Winterthurer Stadtorchester
Conductor: Rudolf Moralt
◇ Verdi: *La Traviata*, "Ah ! fors'è lui" and "Sempre libera" —
Donizetti: *Lucia di Lammermoor*, "Ardon gli incensi . . . Spargi
d'amaro pianto" — Wagner: *Tristan und Isolde*, "Liebestod"

26 June   *Lucia di Lammermoor* by Gaetano Donizetti Radio
broadcast   Rome, RAI Studios
RAI Orchestra and Chorus, Rome
Conductor: Tullio Serafin
M. Callas (Lucia), E. Fernandi (Edgardo), R. Panerai (Enrico)

4, 6 July   *La Sonnambula* by Vincenzo Bellini   Cologne,
opera house
Conductor: Tullio Serafin
Director: Luchino Visconti
M. Callas (Amina), N. Monti (Elvino), N. Zaccaria (Rodolfo)

5 August   **Concert**   Athens, Herodes Atticus Theater
Festival of Athens Orchestra
Conductor: Antonino Votto
◇ Verdi: *Il Trovatore*, "D'amor sull'ali rosee — Verdi: *La Forza del
Destino*, "Pace, pace mio Dio" — Donizetti:
Lucia di Lammermoor, "Regnava nel silenzio" and "Quando rapito in
estasi" — Wagner: *Tristan und Isolde*, "Liebestod" — Thomas:
Hamlet, "A vos jeux, mes amis" and second part of Ophelia's Mad
Scene

19, 21, 26, 29 August   *La Sonnambula* by Vincenzo Bellini
Edinburgh, King's Theatre
Orchestra and choir of La Piccola Scala
Conductor: Antonino Votto
Director: Luchino Visconti
M. Callas (Amina), N. Monti (Elvino), N. Zaccaria (Rodolfo)

21 November   **Concert**   Dallas, State Fair Music Hall
Dallas Symphony Orchestra
Conductor: Nicola Rescigno
◇ Mozart: *Die Entführung aus dem Serail*, "Tutte le torture" —
Bellini: *I Puritani*, "Qui la voce" and "Vien diletto" — Verdi:
Macbeth, "Vien, t'affretta" — Verdi: *La Traviata*, "Ah ! fors'è lui"
— Donizetti: *Anna Bolena*, Mad Scene

7, 10, 16, 19, 22 December   *Un Ballo in Maschera* by Giuseppe
Verdi   Milan, La Scala
Conductor: Gianandrea Gavazzeni
Director: Margherita Wallmann
M. Callas (Amelia), G. di Stefano (Riccardo), E. Bastianini and
R. Roma (Renato), G. Simionato (Ulrica)

31 December   **Television broadcast**   Rome, RAI Studios
◇ Bellini: *Norma*, "Casta diva"

1958

2 January   *Norma* by Vincenzo Bellini   Rome, Opera
Conductor: Gabriele Santini
M. Callas (Norma), F. Corelli (Pollione), M. Pirazzini
(Adalgisa), G. Neri (Oroveso)
Act I only

22 January   **Concert**   Chicago, Lyric Opera
Chicago Symphony Orchestra
Conductor: Nicola Rescigno
◇ Mozart: *Don Giovanni*, "Non mi dir" — Verdi: *Macbeth*,
"Vieni, t'affretta" — Rossini: *Il Barbiere di Siviglia* "Una voce poco
fa" — Boito: *Mefistofele*, "L'altra notte"- Verdi: *Nabucco*, "Anch'io
dischiuso un giorno" — Thomas: *Hamlet*, "A vos jeux, mes amis"

6, 10 February   *La Traviata* by Giuseppe Verdi   New York,
Metropolitan Opera
Conductor: Fausto Cleva
M. Callas (Violetta), D. Barioni and G. Campora
(Alfredo), M. Zanasi (Germont)

13, 20, 25 February   *Lucia di Lammermoor* by Gaetano
Donizetti   New York, Metropolitan Opera
Conductor: Fausto Cleva
M. Callas (Lucia), C. Bergonzi and E. Fernandi
(Edgardo), M. Sereni (Enrico)

28 Februar, 5 March   *Tosca* by Giacomo Puccini   New York,
Metropolitan Opera
Conductor: Dimitri Mitropoulos
M. Callas (Tosca), R. Tucker (Mario), W. Cassel and
G. London (Scarpia)

24 March   **Concert**   Madrid, Cinema Monumental
Orquesta de Camera
Conductor: Giuseppe Morelli
◇ Bellini: *Norma*, "Casta diva" — Verdi: *Il Trovatore*, "D'amor
sull'ali rosee" — Boito: *Mefistofele*, "L'altra notte" — Thomas:
Hamlet, "A vos jeux, mes amis"

27, 30 March   *La Traviata* by Giuseppe Verdi   Lisbon, Teatro
Nacional de São Carlos
Conductor: Franco Ghione
M. Callas (Violetta), A. Kraus (Alfredo), M. Sereni (Germont)

9, 13, 16, 19, 23 April   *Anna Bolena* by Gaetano Donizetti
Milan, La Scala
Conductor: Gianandrea Gavazzeni
M. Callas (Anna Bolena), G. Raimondi (Riccardo), C. Siepi
(Enrico), G. Simionato (Seymour)

19, 22, 25, 28, 31 May   *Il Pirata* by Vincenzo Bellini   Milan,
La Scala
Conductor: Antonino Votto
M. Callas (Imogene), F. Corelli (Gualtiero),
E. Bastianini (Ernesto)

10 June   **Concert**   London, Covent Garden
M. Callas, F. Robertson, J. Shaw, and others
Conductor: John Pritchard
◇ Bellini: *I Puritani*, "Qui la voce" and "Vien dilletto"

17 June   **Television concert**   London, Chelsea Empire Theatre,
BBC
Maria Callas and others
Conductor: John Pritchard
◇ Puccini: *Tosca*, "Vissi d'arte" — Rossini: *Il Barbiere di Siviglia*,
"Una voce poco fa"

20, 23, 26, 28, 30 June *La Traviata* by Giuseppe Verdi
London, Covent Garden
Conductor: Nicola Rescigno
M. Callas (Violetta), C. Valletti (Alfredo), M. Zanasi
(Germont)

23 September **Television concert** London, Chelsea Empire
Theatre, BBC
Conductor: John Pritchard
◇ Bellini: *Norma*, "Casta diva" — Puccini: *Madame Butterfly*,
"Un bel dì vedremo"

11 October **Concert** Birmingham, Municipal Auditorium
Conductor: Nicola Rescigno
◇ Spontini: *La Vestale*, "Tu che invoco" — Verdi: *Macbeth*,
"Ambizioso spirito" and "Vieni, t'affretta" — Rossini: *Il Barbiere di
Siviglia*, "Una voce poco fa" — Boito: *Mefistofele*, "L'altra notte"
Puccini: *La Bohème*, "Quando me'n vo" — Thomas: *Hamlet*, "A vos
jeux, mes amis" and Ophelia's Mad Scene

14 October **Concert** Atlanta, Municipal Auditorium
Conductor and program as above

17 October **Concert** Montreal, Forum
Conductor and program as above

21 October **Concert** Toronto, Maple Leaf Gardens
Conductor and program as above

31 October ; 2 November *La Traviata* by Giuseppe Verdi
Dallas, State Fair Music Hall
Conductor: Nicola Rescigno
Director: Franco Zeffirelli
M. Callas (Violetta), N. Filacuridi (Alfredo), G. Taddei
(Germont)

6, 8 November *Medea* by Luigi Cherubini Dallas, State Fair
Music Hall
Conductor: Nicola Rescigno
M. Callas (Medea), J. Vickers (Giasone), E. Carron (Glauce),
N. Zaccaria (Creonte), T. Berganza (Neris)

15 November **Concert** Cleveland, Public Music House
Conductor and program as 11 October

18 November **Concert** Detroit, Masonic Auditorium
Conductor and program as 11 October

22 November **Concert** Washington, Constitution Hall
Conductor and program as 11 October

26 November **Concert** San Francisco, Civic Auditorium
Conductor and program as 11 October

29 November **Concert** Los Angeles, Shrine Auditorium
Conductor and program as 11 October

19 December **Concert** Paris, Opéra
Maria Callas, Albert Lance and Tito Gobbi
Conductor: Georges Sebastian
Bellini: *Norma*, "Casta diva" — Verdi: *Il Trovatore*, "D'amor sull'ali
rosee" and "Miserere" — Rossini: *Il Barbiere di Siviglia*, "Una voce
poco fa" — Puccini: *Tosca*, Act II

1959

11 January **Concert** St. Louis, Kiel Auditorium
Conductor and program as 11 October 1958

24 January **Concert** Philadelphia, Academy of Music
Philadelphia Philharmonic Orchestra
Conductor: Eugene Ormandy
◇ Boito: *Mefistofele*, "L'altra notte" — Rossini: *Il Barbiere di
Siviglia*, "Una voce poco fa" — Thomas: *Hamlet*, "A vos jeux, mes
amis" and Ophelia's Mad Scene

27 January *Il Pirata* (concert performance) by Vincenzo Bellini
New York, Carnegie Hall
Conductor: Nicola Rescigno
M. Callas (Imogene), P. Miranda Ferraro (Gualtiero),
C. Ego (Ernesto)

29 January *Il Pirata* (concert performance) by Vincenzo Bellini
Washington, Constitution Hall
As above

2 May **Concert** Madrid, Teatro de la Zarzuela
Conductor: Nicola Rescigno
◇ Mozart: *Don Giovanni*, "Non mi dir" — Verdi: *Macbeth*, "Nel
dì della vittoria" and "Vieni, t'affretta" — Rossini: *Semiramide*,
"Nel raggio lusinghier" Ponchielli: *La Gioconda*, "Suicidio!" —
Bellini: *Il Pirata*, Final Scene

5 May **Concert** Barcelona, Gran Teatro del Liceo
Orquesta Sinfonica del Liceo
Conductor: Nicola Rescigno
◇ Verdi: *Don Carlo*, "Tu che le vanità" — Boito: *Mefistofele*,
"L'altra notte" — Rossini: *Il Barbiere di Siviglia*, "Una voce poco fa"
Puccini: *Tosca*, "Vissi d'arte" — Puccini: *La Bohème*, "Quando me
n'vo" — Thomas: *Hamlet*, Final Scene and Ophelia's Mad Scene

15 May **Concert** Hamburg, Musikhalle
Symphonieorchester des Norddeutschen Rundfunks
Conductor: Nicola Rescigno
◇ Spontini: *La Vestale*, "Tu che invoco" — Verdi: *Macbeth*, "Nel
dì della vittoria" — Rossini: *Il Barbiere di Siviglia*, "Una voce poco
fa" — Verdi: *Don Carlo*, "Tu che le vanità" — Bellini: *Il Pirata*,
Final Scene

19 May **Concert** Stuttgart, Liederhalle
Conductor and programme as above

21 May **Concert** Munich, Kongress-Saal
Conductor and program as above

24 May **Concert** Wiesbaden, Kursaal
Conductor and program as above

17, 22, 24, 27, 30 June *Medea* by Luigi Cherubini London,
Covent Garden
Conductor: Nicola Rescigno
M. Callas (Medea), J. Vickers (Giasone), J. Carlyle (Glauce),
N. Zaccaria (Creonte), F. Cossotto (Neris)

11 July **Concert** Amsterdam, Concertgebouw
Concertgebouw Orchestra
Conductor: Nicola Rescigno
◇ Spontini: *La Vestale*, "Tu che invoco" — Verdi: *Ernani*,
"Ernani, Ernani, involami" — Verdi: *Don Carlo*, "Tu che le
vanità" — Bellini: *Il Pirata*, Final Scene

14 July **Concert** Brussels, Théâtre de la Monnaie
Orchestre de la Monnaie
Conductor and program as above

17 September **Concert** Bilbao, Coliseo Albia
Orquesta Sinfonica del Liceo, Barcelona
Conductor: Nicola Rescigno
◇ Verdi: *Don Carlo*, "Tu che le vanità" — Thomas: *Hamlet*,
"A vos jeux, mes amis" — Verdi: *Ernani*, "Ernani, Ernani,
involami" — Bellini: *Il Pirata*, "Col sorriso
d'innocenza"

23 September **Concert** London, Royal Festival Hall
Conductor: Nicola Rescigno
◇ Verdi: *Don Carlo*, "Tu che le vanità" — Bellini: *Il Pirata*,
"Col sorriso d'innocenza" — Thomas: *Hamlet*, A vos jeux, mes
amis" — Verdi: *Macbeth*, "Una macchia è qui tutt'ora"

3 October **Television concert** (broadcast 7 October) London, Wood Green Empire
Royal Philharmonic Orchestra
Conductor: Malcolm Sargent
◇ Puccini: *La Bohème*, "Sì, mi chiamano Mimì" — Boito: *Mefistofele*, "L'altra notte"

23 October **Concert** Berlin, Titania Palast
Berlin Radio Symphony Orchester
Conductor: Nicola Rescigno
◇ Mozart: *Don Giovanni*, "Non mi dir" — Verdi: *Ernani*, "Ernani, Ernani, involami" — Verdi: *Don Carlo*, "Tu che le vanità" — Bellini: *Il Pirata*, "A vos jeux, mes amis" and Mad Scene

28 October **Concert** Kansas City, Midland Theater Kansas City Symphony Orchestra
Conductor: Nicola Rescigno
◇ Mozart: *Don Giovanni*, "Non mi dir" — Donizetti: *Lucia di Lammermoor*, "Regnava nel silenzio" and "Quando rapito in estasi" Verdi: *Ernani*, "Ernani, Ernani, involami" — Bellini: *Il Pirata*, Final Scene

6, 8 November ***Lucia di Lammermoor*** by Gaetano Donizetti
Dallas, State Fair Music Hall
Conductor: Nicola Rescigno
M. Callas (Lucia), G. Raimondi (Edgardo), E. Bastianini (Enrico), N. Zaccaria (Raimondo)

19, 21 November ***Medea*** by Luigi Cherubini Dallas, State Fair Music Hall
Conductor: Nicola Rescigno
M. Callas (Medea), J. Vickers (Giasone), K. Williams (Glauce), N. Zaccaria (Creonte), N. Merriman (Neris)

1960

24, 28 August ***Norma*** by Vincenzo Bellini Epidaurus, ancient theater Greek National Opera Orchestra
Conductor: Tullio Serafin
M. Callas (Norma), M. Picchi (Pollione), K. Morfoniou (Adalgisa), F. Mazzoli (Oroveso)

7, 10, 12, 14, 18, 21 December ***Poliuto*** by Gaetano Donizetti
Milan, La Scala
Conductor: Antonino Votto and Antonio Tonini
M. Callas (Paolina), F. Corelli (Poliuto), E. Bastianini (Severo), N. Zaccaria (Callistene), P. de Palma (Nearco)

1961

30 May **Concert** London, St. James's Palace
Conductor: Malcolm Sargent
◇ Bellini : *Norma*, "Casta diva" — Massenet: *Le Cid*, "Pleurez mes yeux" — Verdi: *Don Carlo*, "Tu che le vanità" — Boito: *Mefistofele*, "L'altra notte"

6, 13 August ***Medea*** by Luigi Cherubini Epidaurus, ancient theater Greek National Opera Orchestra and Chorus
Conductor: Nicola Rescigno
M. Callas (Medea), J. Vickers (Giasone), S. Glantzi (Glauce), G. Modesti (Creonte), K. Morfoniou (Neris)

11, 14, 20 December ***Medea*** by Luigi Cherubini
Milan, La Scala
Conductor: Thomas Schippers
M. Callas (Medea), J. Vickers (Giasone), I. Tosini (Glauce), N. Ghiaurov (Creonte), G. Simionato (Neris)

1962

27 February **Concert** London, Royal Festival Hall
London Philharmonic Orchestra
Conductor: Georges Prêtre

◇ Weber: *Oberon*, "Ocean, Thou mighty monster" — Massenet: *Le Cid*, "Pleurez mes yeux" — Rossini: *La Cenerentola*, "Nacqui al'affanno e al pianto" — Verdi: *Macbeth*, "La luce langue" — Verdi: *Don Carlo*, "Oh don fatale" Donizetti: *Anna Bolena*, "Al dolce guidami"

12 March **Concert** Munich, Kongress-Saal
Bayerisches Staatsorchester
Conductor: Georges Prêtre
◇ Massenet: *Le Cid*, "Pleurez mes yeux" — Bizet: *Carmen*, "Habanera and Seguidilla" — Verdi: *Ernani*, "Sorta è la notte" and "Ernani, Ernani involami" Rossini: *La Cenerentola*, "Nacqui al'affanno e al pianto" — Verdi: *Don Carlo*, "Oh don fatale"

16 March **Concert** Hamburg, Musikhalle
Symphonieorchester des Norddeutschen Rundfunks
Conductor and program as above

19 March **Concert** Essen, Saalbau
Orchester der Stadt Essen
Conductor and program as above

23 March **Concert** Bonn, Beethoven-Halle
Niedersächsisches Symphonieorchester
Conductor and program as above

19 May **Concert** New York, Madison Square Garden
Pianist: Charles Wilson
◇ Bizet: *Carmen*, "Habanera" and "Séguidilla"

29 May ; 3 June ***Medea*** by Luigi Cherubini Milan, La Scala
Conductor: Thomas Schippers
M. Callas (Medea), J. Vickers (Giasone), N. Ghiaurov (Creonte), B. Rizzoli (Glauce), C. Simionato (Neris)

4 November **Television broadcast** London, Covent Garden
Maria Callas and Giuseppe di Stefano, Micha Ellmann, Juliette Gréco, and others
Conductor: Georges Prêtre
◇ Verdi: *Don Carlo*, "Tu che le vanità" — Bizet: *Carmen* "Habanera" and "Séguidilla"

1963

17 May **Concert** Berlin, Deutsche Oper
Orchester der Deutschen Oper, Berlin
Conductor: Georges Prêtre
◇ Rossini: *Semiramide*, "Bel raggio lusinghier" — Bellini: *Norma*, "Casta diva" and "Ah ! bello, a me ritorna" — Verdi: *Nabucco*, "Ben io t'invenni" and "Anch'io dischiuso un giorno" — Puccini: *La Bohème*, "Quando me'n vo" — Puccini: *Madame Butterfly*, "Con onor muore" and "Tu, tu piccolo iddio"

20 May **Concert** Düsseldorf, Rheinhalle
Niedersächsisches Sinfonieorchester
Conductor and program as above

23 May **Concert** Stuttgart, Liederhalle
Symphonieorchester des Südfunks
Conductor and program as above

31 May **Concert** London, Royal Festival Hall
London Philharmonic Orchestra
Conductor and program as above

5 June **Concert** Paris, Théâtre des Champs-Élysées
Orchestre Philharmonique de la RTF
Conductor: Georges Prêtre
◇ Rossini: *Semiramide*, "Nel raggio lusinghier" — Rossini: *La Cenerentola*, "Nacqui all'affanno" and "Al pianto" — Massenet: *Manon Lescaut*, "Adieu notre petite table" — Massenet: *Werther*, "Air des lettres" — Verdi: *Nabucco*, "Ben io t'invenni" and "Anch'io dischiuso un giorno" — Puccini: *La Bohème*, "Quando me'n vo" — Puccini: *Madame Butterfly*, "Tu, tu piccolo iddio" — Puccini: *Gianni Schicchi*, "O mio babbino caro"

9 June   **Concert**   Copenhagen, Falkoner Centret
Danmarks Radiosimfoni Orkester
Conductor and program as 17 May

1964

21, 24, 27, 30 January ; 1, 5 February   *Tosca* by Giacomo
Puccini   London, Covent Garden
Conductor: Carlo Felice Cillario
Director: Franco Zeffirelli
M. Callas (Tosca), R. Cioni (Mario), T. Gobbi (Scarpia)

9 February   *Tosca* (television broadcast) by Giacomo Puccini
London, Covent Garden
Conductor and cast as above
Act II

22, 25, 31 May ; 6, 10, 14, 19, 24 June   *Norma* by Vincenzo
Bellini   Paris, Opéra
Conductor: Georges Prêtre
M. Callas (Norma), C. Craig and F. Corelli (Pollione),
F. Cossotto (Adalgisa), I. Vinco (Oroveso)

1965

19, 22, 26 February ; 1, 3, 5, 8, 10, 13 March   *Tosca* by
Giacomo Puccini   Paris, Opéra
Conductor: Georges Prêtre and Nicola Rescigno
Director: Franco Zeffirelli
M. Callas (Tosca), R. Cioni (Mario), T. Gobbi (Scarpia)

19, 25 March   *Tosca* by Giacomo Puccini   New York,
Metropolitan Opera
Conductor: Fausto Cleva
Director: Franco Zeffirelli
M. Callas (Tosca), F. Corelli (Mario), T. Gobbi (Scarpia)

14, 17, 21, 24, 29 May   *Norma* by Vincenzo Bellini
Paris, Opéra
Conductor: Georges Prêtre
M. Callas (Norma), G. Cecchele (Pollione), G. Simionato and
F. Cossotto (Adalgisa), I. Vinco (Oroveso)

18 May   **Television broadcast**   Paris, RTF Studio
Orchestre Nationale de la RTF
Conductor: Georges Prêtre
◇ Massenet: *Manon Lescaut*, "Adieu notre petite table" —
Bellini: *La Sonnambula*, "Ah ! non credea" — Puccini: *Gianni
Schicchi*, "O mio babbino caro"

5 July   *Tosca* by Giacomo Puccini   London, Covent Garden
Conductor: Georges Prêtre
Director: Franco Zeffirelli
M. Callas (Tosca), R. Cioni (Mario), T. Gobbi (Scarpia)

1969

June and July   Filming of *Medea*   Turkey: Goremme — Syria:
Aleppo — Italy: Grado, Pisa, Rome
Director: Pier Paolo Pasolini
Producer: Roberto Rossellini
M. Callas (Medea), G. Gentile (Giasone), L. Terzieff
(Centauro)
Premiere: Rome, 9 January 1970

1971

11 October—18 November   **Master classes**   New York, Julliard
School of Music

1972

7 February—16 March   **Master classes**   New York, Julliard
School of Music

1973

10 April   *Les Vêpres Siciliennes* by Giuseppe Verdi   Turin,
Teatro Regio
Director: Maria Callas and Giuseppe di Stefano

25 October   **Farewell concert tour**   Hamburg,
Kongresszentrum
Maria Callas and Giuseppe di Stefano
Pianist: Ivor Newton
Varying program chosen from the following arias:
Massenet : *Le Cid* "Pleurez mes yeux" — Bizet: *Carmen*,
"Habanera" — Ponchielli: *La Gioconda*, "Suicidio !" — Boito:
Mefistofele, "L'altra notte" — Verdi: *Don Carlo*, "Non pianger mia
compagna" and "Tu che le vanità" — Verdi: *Les Vêpres Siciliennes*,
"Mercé dilette amiche" — Puccini: *Gianni Schicchi*, "O mio
babbino caro" — Puccini: *La Bohème*, "Quando me'n vo" —
Puccini: *Manon Lescaut*, "In quelle trine morbide" and "Sola,
perduta, abbandonata"
Duets:
Bizet: *Carmen*, "C'est toi, c'est moi" — Donizetti: *L'Elisir d'Amore*,
"Una parola, o Adina" — Verdi: *La Forza del Destino*, "Ah per
sempre" — Verdi: *Don Carlo*, "Io vengo a domandar" —
Mascagni: *Cavalleria Rusticana*, "Tu qui, Santuzza ?" — Verdi: *Les
Vêpres Siciliennes*, "Quale, o prode"

29 October   **Farewell concert tour**   Berlin, Philharmonie
Maria Callas and Giuseppe di Stefano
Pianist and program as above

2 November   **Farewell concert tour**   Düsseldorf, Rheinhalle
Maria Callas and Giuseppe di Stefano
Pianist and program as above

6 November   **Farewell concert tour**   Munich, Kongress-Saal
Maria Callas and Giuseppe di Stefano
Pianist and program as above

9 November   **Farewell concert tour**   Frankfurt, Jahrhunderthalle
Maria Callas and Giuseppe di Stefano
Pianist and program as above

12 November   **Farewell concert tour**   Mannheim,
Nationaltheater
Maria Callas and Giuseppe di Stefano
Pianist and program as above

20 November   **Farewell concert tour**   Madrid, Palacio Nacional
de Congresos
Maria Callas and Giuseppe di Stefano
Pianist and program as above

26 November, 2 December   **Farewell concert tour**   London,
Royal Festival Hall
Maria Callas and Giuseppe di Stefano
Pianist and program as above

8 December   **Farewell concert tour**   Paris, Théâtre des Champs-
Élysées
Maria Callas and Giuseppe di Stefano
Pianist and program as above

11 October—18 November   **Master classes**   New York, Julliard
School of Music

11 December   **Farewell concert tour**   Amsterdam,
Concertgebouw
Maria Callas and Giuseppe di Stefano
Pianist and program as above

1974

20 January   **Farewell concert tour**   (private performance) Milan,
Istituto del Cancro
Maria Callas and Giuseppe di Stefano
Pianist and program as above
In addition: Mascagni: *Cavalleria Rusticana*, "Voi lo sapete,
o mamma" — Puccini: *Tosca*, "Vissi d'arte" — Massenet: *Werther*,
"Air des lettres" — Massenet: *Manon Lescaut*, "Adieu notre petite
table"

23 January   **Farewell concert tour**   Stuttgart, Liederhalle
Maria Callas (performance cancelled due to Giuseppe di
Stefanos falling ill)
Pianist: Ivor Newton
◇ Maria Callas sang Puccini instead: *Gianni Schicchi*, "O mio
babbino caro"

11 February   **Farewell concert tour**   Philadelphia, Academy
of Music
Maria Callas and Giuseppe di Stefano
Pianist and program as 20 January

21 February   **Farewell concert tour**   Toronto, Massey Hall
Maria Callas and Giuseppe di Stefano
Pianist and program as 20 January

24 February   **Farewell concert tour**   Washington,
Constitution Hall
Maria Callas and Giuseppe di Stefano
Pianist and program as 20 January

27 February   **Farewell concert tour**   Boston, Symphony Hall
Maria Callas (without Giuseppe di Stefano, due to an illness)
Pianist: Vasso Devetzi
Program as 20 January

2 March   **Farewell concert tour**   Chicago, Civic Opera
Maria Callas and Giuseppe di Stefano
Pianist and program as above

5 March   **Farewell concert tour**   New York, Carnegie Hall
Maria Callas and Giuseppe di Stefano
Pianist and program as 20 January

9 March   **Farewell concert tour**   Detroit, Masonic Auditorium
Maria Callas (without Giuseppe di Stefano, due to an illness)
Pianist: R. Votapek
Program as 20 January

21 March   **Farewell concert tour**   Dallas, State Fair Music Hall
Maria Callas (without Giuseppe di Stefano, due to an illness)
Pianist: Earl Wild
Program as 20 January

4 April   **Farewell concert tour**   Ohio, Columbus Theatre
Maria Callas and Giuseppe di Stefano
Pianist and program as 20 January

9 April   **Farewell concert tour**   Brookville, Long Island, Post
Center Auditorium
Maria Callas and Giuseppe di Stefano
Pianist and program as 20 January

15 April   **Farewell concert tour**   New York, Carnegie Hall
Maria Callas and Giuseppe di Stefano
Pianist and program as 20 January

24 April   **Farewell concert tour**   Seattle, Opera House
Maria Callas and Giuseppe di Stefano
Pianist and program as 20 January

25 April   **Farewell concert tour**   Portland, Civic Auditorium
Maria Callas and Giuseppe di Stefano
Pianist and program as 20 January

1 May   **Farewell concert tour**   Vancouver, Queen Elizabeth
Theatre
Maria Callas and Giuseppe di Stefano
Pianist and program as 20 January

5 May   **Farewell concert tour**   Los Angeles, Shrine Auditorium
Maria Callas and Giuseppe di Stefano
Pianist and program as 20 January

9 May   **Farewell concert tour**   San Francisco, War Memorial
Opera House
Maria Callas and Giuseppe di Stefano
Pianist and program as 20 January

13 May   **Farewell concert tour**   Montreal, Palais des Arts
Maria Callas and Giuseppe di Stefano
Pianist: Ivor Newton
Program as 20 January

5, 8 October   **Farewell concert tour**   Seoul
Maria Callas and Giuseppe di Stefano
Pianist and program as 20 January

12, 19, 27 October   **Farewell concert tour**   Tokyo, NHK
Maria Callas and Giuseppe di Stefano
Pianist and program as 20 January

24 October   **Farewell concert tour**   Osaka
Maria Callas and Giuseppe di Stefano
Pianist and program as 20 January

7 November   **Farewell concert tour**   Hiroshima
Maria Callas and Giuseppe di Stefano
Pianist and program as 20 January

11 November   **Farewell concert tour**   Sapporo
Maria Callas and Giuseppe di Stefano
Pianist and program as 20 January

Bibliography

Ardoin, John. *The Callas Legacy*. London 1979

Ardoin, John and Gerald Fitzgerald. *Callas*. New York 1974

Ardoin, John, ed. *Callas at Juilliard*. New York 1987

Bing, Rudolf. *5000 Nights at the Opera*. New York 1972

Callas, Evangelia. *My Daughter — Maria Callas*. New York 1960

Callas, Jackie. *Sisters*. London 1989

Cederna, Camilla. *Chi è Maria Callas?* Milan 1968

Gastel, Chiarelli, Christina. *Callas*. Venice 1981

Galatopoulos, Stelios. *Callas, La Divina*. London 1963

Gara, Eugenio. *Le grandi interpreti — Maria Callas*. Milan 1957

Gobbi, Tito. *My Life*. London 1984

Guandalini, Gina. *Callas — L'ultima diva*. Torino 1987

Herzfeld, Friedrich. *La Callas*. Berlin 1959

Jellinek, George. *Callas. Portrait of a Prima Donna*. New York 1960

Kesting, Jürgen. *Maria Callas*. Düsseldorf 1990

Lauri-Volpi, Giacomo. *Voci parallele*. Milan 1955

Lowe, David A. *Callas — As They Saw Her*. London 1987

Lorcey, Jacques. *Maria Callas — D'art et d'amour*. Paris 1983

Marchand, Polyvios. *Maria Callas*. Athens 1983

Maxwell, Elsa. *I Married the World*. London 1955

Menechini, Giovanni Battista. *Maria Callas mia moglie*. Milan 1981

Merlin, Olivier. *Le Bel Canto*. Paris 1961

Monestier, Martin. *Maria Callas — le livre du souvenir*. Paris 1985

Picchetti, Maria Teresa and Marta Teglia. *El arte de Maria Callas como metalenguaje*. Buenos Aires 1969

Rémi, Pierre-Jean. *Maria Callas — A Tribute*. New York 1987

Riemens, Leo. *Maria Callas*. Utrecht 1960

La Rochelle, Réal. *Callas — la diva et le vinyle*. Montréal 1987

Scott, Michael. *Maria Meneghini Callas*. London 1991

Segalini, Sergio. *Callas. Les images d'une voix*. Paris 1979

Stancioff, Nadia. *Maria — Callas Remembered*. New York 1987

Stassinopoulos, Arianna. *Maria — Beyond the Callas Legend*. London 1980

Winbeski, Henri. *Maria Callas: The Art behind the Legend*. New York 1975

Zeffirelli, Franco. *The Autobiography of Franco Zeffirelli*. London 1986

Articles

Anonymous. "Maria Callas — The Prima Donna." *Time* 44. 1956

Anonymous. "Maria Callas — Die Primadonna." *Der Spiegel* 7. 1957

Anonymous. "Maria Callas: Memoires." *Oggi*. January/February 1957

Anonymous. "The Callas Debate." *Opera*. September/October 1970

Ardoin, John. "Callas Today." *Musical America*. December 1964

Ardoin, John. "The Kelly Years." *Opera News*. November 1974

Ardoin, John. "The Callas Legacy Updated." *Opera News*. August 1978

Barnes, Clive. "Callas the Unique." *Music and Musicians*. January 1964

Bachmann, Ingeborg. "Hommage à Maria Callas. Draft." In *Die Wahrheit ist dem Menschen zumutbar*. Serie Piper 218. Munich 1978

Cassidy, Claudia. "Splendor in the Night: Callas Remembered." *Opera News*. November 1977

Clark, Robert S. "Learning from Callas." *Stereo Review*. March 1972

DuPond, Carlos Diaz. "Callas in Mexico." *Opera*. April 1973

Greenfield, Edward. "Art of Maria Callas." *High Fidelity*. March 1964

Hamilton, David. "The Recordings of Maria Callas." *High Fidelity*. March 1974

Hamilton, David. "Who Speaks for Callas?" *High Fidelity*. January 1979

Harewood, Earl of. "The Art of Maria Callas." *Recorded Sound*. October 1979

Heinsen, Geerd. "Aufgelegt. Maria Callas auf CD — Erbe und Distanz." *Orpheus*. October 1987

Legge, Walter. "La Divina. Callas Remembered." *Opera News*. November 1977

Leibowitz, René. "Le secret de la Callas." *Temps modernes*. July 1959

Maguire, Jan. "Callas, Serafin, and the Art of Bel Canto." *Saturday Review*. 30 March 1968

Neville, Robert. "Voice of an Angel." *Life*. 31 October 1955

Osborne, Conrad. "The Callas Master Classes." *Musical America*. June 1972

Rizzo, Francis. "The Callas Class." *Opera News*. April 1972

Rosenthal, Harold, Carlo Maria Giulini, Tito Gobbi, Lord Harewood, Rolf Liebermann, John Tooley, Margherita Wallmann et al. "Callas Remembered." *Opera*. November 1977

Saal, Hubert. "Callas on the Record." *Newsweek*. 15 February 1971

Schonberg, Harald. "Callas at the Met." *Show*. May 1965

Scorr, Michael. "A Connoisseur's Callas." *Opera News*. September 1987

Schroeter, Werner. "Der Herztod der Primadonna." *Der Spiegel* 40. 1977

Soria, Dorle S. "Greek Sorceress." *Opera News*. November 1977

Voigt, Thomas. "Demonstrationen konkurrenzloser Vielseitigkeit." *Fono Forum*. September 1987

Photo Credits

A Schirmer/Mosel Production

Copyright © 1995 by Schirmer/Mosel Verlag, Munich, Germany

Published in 1996 and distributed in the U.S. by
Stewart, Tabori and Chang, a division of U.S. Media Holdings, Inc.
575 Broadway, New York, New York 10012

Distributed in Canada by General Publishing Co. Ltd.
30 Lesmill Road, Don Mills, Ontario, Canada, M3B 2T6.
Distributed in Australia and New Zealand by Peribo Pty Ltd.,
59 Beaumont Road, Mount Kuring-gai, NSW 2080, Australia.
Sold in Southeast Asia by R & S Summers, Ralph and Sheila
Summers, 26 Monkhams Drive, Woodford Green, Essex IG8 0LQ, England.

Translated from the German by Anne Heritage.

ISBN: 1-55670-483-6

Library of Congress Catalog Card Number: 96-67554

10 9 8 7 6 5 4 3 2 1

First Edition

Printed in Germany